THE TRUTH ABOUT
MANAGING PEOPLE

THIRD EDITION

Stephen P. Robbins

Printed in the United States of America

First Printing: October 2012

ISBN-10: 0-13-309044-2
ISBN-13: 978-0-13-309044-4

Pearson Education LTD.
Pearson Education Australia PTY, Limited.
Pearson Education Singapore, Pte. Ltd.
Pearson Education North Asia, Ltd.
Pearson Education Canada, Ltd.
Pearson Educación de Mexico, S.A. de C.V.
Pearson Education—Japan
Pearson Education Malaysia, Pte. Ltd.

*The Library of Congress cataloging-in-publication data
is on file.*

Vice President, Publisher
Tim Moore

**Associate Publisher and
Director of Marketing**
Amy Neidlinger

Acquisitions Editor
Jeanne Glasser Levine

Editorial Assistant
Pamela Boland

Operations Specialist
Jodi Kemper

Marketing Manager
Megan Graue

**Cover and Interior
Designs**
Stuart Jackman
Dorling Kindersley

Design Manager
Sandra Schroeder

Managing Editor
Kristy Hart

Project Editor
Jovana San Nicolas-Shirley

Copy Editor
Chuck Hutchinson

Proofreader
Sheri Cain

Senior Compositor
Gloria Schurick

Manufacturing Buyer
Dan Uhrig

For my wife Laura

Preface

Managers are bombarded with advice from consultants, professors, business journalists, and assorted management "gurus" on how to manage their employees. A lot of this advice is well researched and valuable. Much of it, however, is a gross generalization, ambiguous, inconsistent, or superficial. Some of it is even just downright wrong. Regardless of the quality, there doesn't seem to be any slowdown in the outpouring of this advice. Quite the contrary. Books on business and management have replaced sex, self-help, and weight loss as topics on many nonfiction best-sellers' lists. Sadly, most of these books are not evidence-based. Most, in fact, seem to be oblivious to the wealth of research on managing people at work and rely on personal opinions, limited experience, or unsupported observations. If you want evidence of this, look at some of the titles in the "Leadership" section of your local bookstore. You'll find titles like *The Leadership Secrets of Attila the Hun; Make It So: Leadership Lessons from Star Trek; The Leadership Secrets of Santa Claus;* and *Toy Box Leadership: Leadership Lessons from the Toys You Loved as a Child.*

I've been teaching and writing about managing people at work for more than 40 years. As part of my writing efforts, I have read upwards of 30,000 research studies on human behavior. While my practitioner friends are often quick to criticize research and theory-testing, this research has provided us with innumerable insights into human behavior. Unfortunately, there has been no short, concise summary of behavioral research that cuts through the jargon to give managers the truth about what works and doesn't work when it comes to managing people at work. Well, that's no longer true since the first edition of this book.

As with the previous editions, I've organized this book around key, human-behavior-related problem areas that managers face: hiring, motivation, leadership, communication, team building, performance evaluation, and coping with change. Within each problem area, I've identified a select set of topics that are relevant to managers and where there is substantial research evidence to draw upon. I've also included suggestions to help readers apply this information to improve their managerial effectiveness. Sixteen topics are new to this edition, and the others have been updated. **New to this edition are contemporary topics such as ethical leadership, virtual leadership, the dark side of charisma, organizational citizenship behavior, age stereotypes, organizational politics, digital distractions at work, the motivational power of recognition, and managing layoff-survivor sickness.**

Who is this book written for? Practicing managers and those aspiring to a management position—from CEOs to supervisor wannabes. I wrote it because I believe you shouldn't have to read through detailed textbooks in human resources or organizational behavior to learn the truth about managing people at work. Nor should you have to attend an executive development course at a prestigious university to get the straight facts. What you get from this book, of course, will depend on your current knowledge about organizational behavior. Recent MBAs, for instance, will find this book to be a concise summary of the evidence they spent many months studying. They won't see elaborated theories or names of major researchers but they will find accurate translations of research findings. For individuals who haven't kept current with research in organizational behavior or for those with little formal academic training, this book should provide a wealth of new insights into managing people at work.

You'll find each of the 59 topics in this book is given its own short chapter. And each chapter is essentially independent from the others. You can read them in any order you desire. Best of all, you needn't tackle this book in one sitting. It's been designed for multiple "quick reads." Read a few chapters, put it down, then pick it up again at a later date. There's no continuous story line that has to be maintained.

Let me conclude this preface by stating the obvious: A book is a team project. While there is only one name on the cover, a number of people contributed to getting this book in your hands. That team included Tim Moore, Jeanne Glasser Levine, Jovana San Nicolas-Shirley, and Amy Neidlinger. My thanks to each.

Stephen P. Robbins

TRUTH

1

First Impressions DO Count!

When we meet someone for the first time, we notice a number of things about that person—physical characteristics, clothes, firmness of handshake, gestures, tone of voice, and the like. We then use these impressions to fit the person into ready-made categories. And this early categorization, formed quickly and on the basis of minimal information, tends to hold greater weight than impressions and information received later. This categorization is what we commonly refer to as a first impression.

Psychologists refer to the power of first impressions as the primacy effect. Essentially, it just means that first impressions influence latter impressions. What's important from our perspective is that the primacy effect carries a lot of weight when we assess other people and, maybe more importantly, that first impressions of people are not very accurate.

Why do we rely so heavily on first impressions? Basically, we're looking for a shortcut. When we meet new people, we want to categorize them so that we can process and understand information about them quickly. The error is compounded by the fact that we tend to cling to our first impressions. When later information is received that might contradict that first impression, we tend to discount, misrepresent, reinterpret, or even ignore it.

The best evidence on first impressions comes from research on employment interviews. Findings clearly demonstrate that first impressions count. More specifically, the information processed first has a greater effect on later judgments than subsequent information does.

Research on applicant appearance confirms the power of first impressions. Studies have looked at assessments made of applicants before the actual interview—that brief period in which the applicant walks into an interview room, exchanges greetings with the

When later information is received that might contradict our first impression, we tend to discount, misrepresent, reinterpret, or even ignore it.

interviewer, sits down, and engages in minor chit-chat. The evidence indicates that the way applicants walk, talk, dress, and look can have a great impact on the interviewer's evaluation of applicant qualifications. Facial attractiveness seems to be particularly influential. Applicants who are highly attractive are evaluated as more qualified for a variety of jobs than those who are unattractive.

Initial positive impressions even reshape the interview itself. Positive first impressions lead interviewers to speak in a more pleasant interpersonal style and to ask less-threatening questions.

A final body of confirmative research finds that interviewers' post-interview evaluations of applicants conform, to a substantial degree, to their pre-interview impressions. That is, those first impressions carry considerable weight in shaping the interviewers' final evaluations, regardless of what actually transpired in the interview itself. This latter conclusion assumes that the interview elicits no highly negative information.

Based on numerous studies of the interview process, we can say that first impressions are powerful influences on outcomes. Instead of using the interviews to gather unbiased information, interviewers typically use the process to merely confirm first impressions.

Can managers do anything to lessen the power of first impressions? Yes. First, we suggest that you avoid the tendency to make quick initial judgments. Try to stay neutral when you meet someone for the first time. The more time that goes by before you make a conclusion, the better you'll know the person and the more accurate your assessment. Second, keep your mind open for new information that may contradict earlier assessments. Think of any early impression as a working hypothesis that you're constantly testing for its accuracy.

> Based on numerous studies of the interview process, we can say that first impressions are powerful influences on outcomes.

TRUTH

2

Forget Traits; It's Behavior That Counts!

You're interviewing applicants to fill a job position in your firm. What are you looking for in these applicants? If you're like many managers, you'll answer with terms such as hardworking, persistent, confident, and dependable. After all, how can you go wrong trying to hire people with traits such as these? Well, you can! The problem is that traits aren't necessarily good predictors of future job performance.

Most of us have a strong belief in the power of traits to predict behavior. We know that people behave differently in different situations, but we tend to classify people by their traits, impose judgments about those traits (being self-assured is "good"; being submissive is "bad"), and make evaluations about people based on these trait classifications. Managers often do this when they make hiring decisions or evaluate current employees. After all, if managers truly believed that situations rather than traits determined behavior, they would hire people almost at random and structure the situation to fit the employee's strengths. But the employee selection process in most organizations places a great deal of emphasis on traits. We see this in the emphasis placed on how applicants perform in interviews and on tests. During interviews, managers watch and listen to see if applicants have the "qualities" they're looking for in a "good" employee. Similarly, tests are often used to determine the degree to which an applicant has "good employee traits."

There are two problems with using traits in the hiring process. First, organizational settings are strong situations that have a large impact on employee behavior. Second, individuals are highly adaptive, and personality traits change in response to organizational situations. Let me elaborate on each of these points.

We tend to classify people by their traits.

The effect of traits in explaining behavior is likely to be strongest in relatively weak situations and weakest in relatively strong situations. Organizational settings tend to be strong situations because they have rules and other formal regulations that define acceptable behavior and punish deviant behavior, and because they have informal norms that dictate appropriate behaviors. These formal and informal constraints minimize the effects of different personality traits. In contrast, picnics, parties, and similar informal functions are weak situations, and we'd predict that traits would be fairly strong predictors of behavior in these situations.

While personality traits are generally stable over time, there is a growing body of evidence that demonstrates that an individual's traits are changed by the organization in which that individual participates. Moreover, people typically belong to multiple organizations (for instance, community, religious, social, athletic, and political, as well as to an employer) that often include very different kinds of members, and they adapt to those different situations. The fact is that people are not prisoners of a rigid and stable personality framework. They can, and do, adjust their behavior to reflect the requirements of various situations.

If traits aren't very good for predicting future employee behavior, what should managers use? The answer is: past behaviors! The best predictor of a person's future behavior is his or her past behavior. So when interviewing candidates, ask questions that focus on previous experiences that are relevant to the current job opening. And ask for actual work experiences rather than hypothetical ones. For instance, ask: "What have you done in previous jobs that demonstrates your creativity?" Or "on your last job, what was it that you most wanted to accomplish but didn't? Why didn't you?" And instead of asking "how *would* you handle situation xyz?" ask "how *did* you handle situation xyz?"

> The best predictor of a person's future behavior is his or her past behavior.

TRUTH

3

Brains Matter; or Why You Should Hire Smart People

Few topics generate more heated discussion and controversy than that of intelligence. People seem to hold widely differing and strong opinions on questions such as: Is IQ a good measure of intelligence? Is intelligence learned or inherited? Are intelligent people more successful than their less-intelligent peers?

We're concerned with the relationship between intelligence (or what is technically referred to as general mental ability) and job performance—specifically, do people with higher intelligence outperform their peers with lower intelligence? Not surprisingly, this is a topic in which there is no shortage of opinions. But don't put much weight on opinions. You should look for hard evidence. And there is actually quite a bit of hard evidence to draw upon. Certain facts are beyond significant technical dispute. For instance: (1) IQ score closely matches whatever it is that people mean when they use the word *intelligent* or *smart* in ordinary language; (2) IQ scores are stable, although not perfectly so, over much of a person's life; (3) properly administered IQ tests are not demonstrably biased against social, economic, ethnic, or racial groups; and (4) smarter employees, on average, are more proficient employees. I understand that some of these conclusions may make you uncomfortable or conflict with your personal views, but they are well supported by the research evidence.

All jobs require the use of intelligence or cognitive ability. Why? For reasoning and decision making. High IQs show a strong correlation with performance in jobs that are novel, ambiguous, changing, or in multifaceted professional occupations such as accountants, engineers, scientists, architects, and physicians. But IQ is also a good predictor in moderately complex jobs, such as crafts, clerical, and police work. IQ is a less valid predictor for unskilled jobs that require only routine decision making or simple problem solving.

> Smarter employees, on average, are more proficient employees.

All jobs require the use of intelligence or cognitive ability.

Intelligence clearly is not the only factor affecting job performance, but it's often the most important. It is, for example, a better predictor of job performance than an employment interview, reference checks, or college transcripts. Unfortunately, the strong genetic component of IQ—probably 70 percent or more of our intelligence is inherited—makes the use of IQ as a selection tool vulnerable to attack. Critics are uncomfortable when average IQs are shown to differ among different races or that IQ has been found to be associated with economic differences. Some critics use these findings to suggest that IQ measures discriminate and, therefore, should be abandoned. This is unfortunate because the evidence overwhelmingly indicates that IQ tests are not biased against particular groups, even though what they measure is largely outside the control of the individual.

Our conclusion: The race may not always go to the swiftest or the strongest, but that's the way to bet! If you want to hire the best possible workforce, all other things being equal, hire the smartest people you can find.

TRUTH

4

When in Doubt, Hire Conscientious People!

We know that people don't have common personalities. Some are quiet and passive; others are loud and aggressive. Some are relaxed; others are tense.

An extensive amount of research has identified five basic dimensions that explain the significant variation in human personality. These five factors are

- **Extraversion**—Are you an extravert (outgoing, sociable) or an introvert (reserved, timid)?

- **Agreeableness**—Are you highly agreeable (cooperative, trusting) or low (disagreeable, antagonistic)?

- **Conscientiousness**—Are you highly conscientious (responsible, organized) or low (unreliable, disorganized)?

- **Emotional stability**—Are you stable (calm, self-confident) or unstable (anxious, insecure)?

- **Openness to experience**—Are you open to new experiences (creative, curious) or closed (conventional, seek the familiar)?

Numerous studies have been undertaken to see if there is any relationship between these five personality dimensions and job performance. Findings indicate that conscientiousness is most related to job performance. Specifically, conscientiousness predicts job performance across a broad spectrum of jobs—from professionals (engineers, accountants, lawyers) to police, salespeople, and semi-skilled workers. Individuals who score high in conscientiousness are dependable, reliable, careful, thorough, able to plan, organized, hardworking, persistent, and achievement-oriented. And these attributes tend to lead to higher job performance in most occupations. Additionally, research indicates that the power of conscientiousness transfers across borders. For instance, a review of studies covering people in 15 European

> Conscientiousness predicts job performance across a broad spectrum of jobs—from professionals to police, salespeople, and semi-skilled workers.

countries found conscientiousness to predict performance across jobs and occupational groups.

So, in contrast to our conclusions in Truth 2, "Forget Traits; It's Behavior That Counts," if you're looking for a single personality characteristic that is likely to be associated with high job performance, you're well advised to try to hire people who score high on conscientiousness. Let me note, however, one interesting caveat: More of this trait is not necessarily better. Evidence indicates that extremely conscientious people typically don't perform any better in their jobs than those who are merely above average.

You're well advised to try to hire people who score high on conscientiousness.

Our conclusions on conscientiousness, of course, don't mean that other characteristics might not be relevant for specific jobs. For instance, evidence indicates that extraversion is a good predictor of performance in managerial and sales positions. This makes sense since these occupations involve high social interaction.

Some readers might be surprised that high emotional stability wasn't found to be related to job performance. Intuitively, it would seem that people who are calm and secure would do better on almost all jobs than people who are anxious and insecure. Closer inspection suggests that only people who have fairly high scores on emotional stability retain their jobs. So the range among those people studied, all of whom were employed, tended to be quite small. In other words, people who are low in emotional stability either don't tend to get hired in the first place or, when they do, they typically don't last too long in their jobs.

5

Want Friendly Employees? It's in the Genes!

Executives at Southwest Airlines recognize what many managers fail to notice: Some people are just inherently more friendly and upbeat than others. Southwest believes, and rightly so, that it's difficult, if not impossible, to train people to provide friendly and courteous service. So Southwest Airlines focuses its hiring process on selecting out people who aren't basically happy and outgoing.

A number of jobs—flight attendants, retail clerks, salespeople, and customer service are some obvious examples—are performed better by people with positive dispositions. Many managers trying to fill these jobs have assumed that pleasant employees can be created. They spend a lot of their time trying to design motivating jobs, working conditions, or attractive compensation and benefit programs to encourage their employees to be friendly and upbeat. Additionally, they spend millions of dollars on training to shape behavior. Most of these programs fail to achieve their objective. Why? Because whether a person is happy or not is essentially determined by his or her genetic structure. Studies have found that 35 to 50 percent, and maybe as much as 80 percent, of people's differences in happiness is attributable to their genes.

One of the more interesting streams of research on this subject has been done by comparing sets of identical twins who were separated at birth and raised apart. If environment were the prime shaper of personality, you'd think that the twins would likely have little in common if they were raised in very different households. But that's not the case. One set of twins, for example, had been separated for 39 years and raised 45 miles apart. Nevertheless, they drove the same model and color of car, chain-smoked the same brand of cigarette, owned dogs with the same name, and regularly vacationed within three blocks of each other at a beach community 1,500 miles away. Evidence like this has led

> Studies have found that 35 to 50 percent, and maybe as much as 80 percent, of people's differences in happiness is attributable to their genes.

researchers to conclude that genetics accounts for about 50 percent of the personality similarities between twins.

Analysis of satisfaction data for individuals over a 50-year period found that individual results were amazingly stable over time, even when these people changed employers and occupations. This analysis and other evidence suggests that an individual's disposition toward life is largely established by his or her genetic makeup, that it holds over time, and carries over into his or her disposition toward work.

The message here is to follow Southwest's example. If you want pleasant employees, focus your attention on the hiring process. Select out the negative, maladjusted, trouble-making fault finders who derive little satisfaction in anything about their jobs. How? Through personality testing, in-depth interviewing, and careful checking of applicant's previous work records.

> An individual's disposition toward life holds over time and carries over into his or her disposition toward work.

TRUTH

6

Realistic Job Previews: What You See Is What You Get

Think back to the last time you went for a job interview. Once the interviewer got past asking you questions, how did he or she describe the job and organization? Most managers, when conducting employment interviews, almost exclusively focus on positive aspects. They talk about interesting work assignments, the camaraderie among coworkers, opportunities for advancement, great benefits, and the like. Even though managers typically know the downside of the job and the organization, they carefully avoid those topics. Why turn off a good job applicant by talking about negatives?

Managers who focus only on the positives are making a mistake. They're setting themselves up for the disappointment of a sudden and surprising resignation. All those hours spent reviewing candidate applications and conducting interviews prove wasted when after only a few weeks or a month into the job, the new employee abruptly quits.

Is there anything an astute manager can do to avoid this experience? The answer is Yes: Use realistic job previews.

Realistic job previews provide job applicants with both unfavorable and favorable information before

> **Managers who focus only on the positives are making a mistake.**

an offer is made. It's in direct contrast to the typical job previews that most managers give during the interview stage—carefully worded descriptions that sell the positive aspects of the new job and the organization. All these do is set up the employee with false expectations. No job or organization is perfect. And you're more likely to keep your new hires if you're straight with them from the beginning.

Why do realistic previews reduce turnover? The evidence indicates that this openness enhances the perception in applicants of the organization's honesty.

When the information that a job applicant receives is excessively inflated, a number of things happen that have potentially negative effects on the organization. First, mismatched applicants who would probably become dissatisfied with the job and soon quit are less likely to select themselves out of the search process. Second, the absence of negative information builds unrealistic expectations. If hired, the new employee is likely to become quickly disappointed. This, in turn, leads to low employee satisfaction and premature resignations. Finally, new hires are prone to becoming disillusioned and less committed to the organization

You're more likely to keep your new hires if you're straight with them from the beginning.

when they come face-to-face with the negatives in the job. No one likes to feel as if he or she was tricked or misled during the hiring process.

A realistic job preview balances both the positive and negative aspects of the job. For instance, in addition to positive comments, managers could tell candidates that there are limited opportunities to talk with coworkers during work hours, or that erratic fluctuations in workloads create considerable stress on employees during rush periods. Anousheh Ansari, chief operating officer at Telecom Technologies, is a proponent of realistic previews. She says she purposely paints a gloomy picture and tries to scare prospective employees during interviews. For example, she tells them that they'll be expected to put in 10- and 12-hour workdays. "Some people run in the opposite direction, but the ones who stay are committed and willing to do whatever it takes," she says.

The evidence indicates that applicants who have been given a realistic job preview hold lower and more realistic expectations about the job they'll be doing and are better prepared for coping with the job and its frustrating elements. The result is fewer unexpected resignations. While presenting only the positive aspects of a job to a recruit may initially entice him or her to join the organization, it may be a marriage that both you and the new employee will quickly regret.

TRUTH

7

Throw Out Your Age Stereotypes

There are numerous age stereotypes about older workers (typically defined as those over age 55)—and most of them are negative. Some of the more popular ones include: Older workers tire more easily; can't learn new skills; lack flexibility; resist change; don't work well with younger bosses; are less productive than younger colleagues; have reduced cognitive abilities; and miss more work days due to illnesses. The truth is that most of these stereotypes are wrong.

Why is it important for managers to overcome any negative stereotypes of older workers? The answer is simply that the workforce is aging and managers can expect to be working with older employees. Even ignoring the legal repercussions from age discrimination, this has important implications for managers. The reality is that the workforce is aging in the U.S. and in other industrial nations. For instance, in the U.S., between 1998 and 2008, civilian workers aged 55 and over increased 49.9 percent compared with just 5.5 percent for those 25–54 and an actual decrease of 2.8 percent for those 16–24. By the year 2015, over 20 percent of the U.S. workforce will be 55 or older. As a manager, you're very likely to be hiring, working with, or working for someone who is older—and holding inaccurate stereotypes can be a serious impediment to that relationship. Now, let's look at the evidence.

Many believe job productivity declines with age. And at first glance, that may seem logical. As we age, our vision and hearing often decline. So do our muscular strength, manual dexterity, and reaction time. But these factors don't necessarily translate into impaired performance because they tend to be offset by experience, judgment, and a strong work ethic.

> The workforce is aging and managers can expect to be working with older employees.

The overall evidence indicates that age and job performance are unrelated. In fact, performance often improves with age and when declines occur, they tend to be small. One likely explanation for why performance increases with age is that older workers tend to have longer job tenure, and increases in job tenure are associated with higher job performance. The evidence also shows that there are much greater differences in job performance within age groups than between age groups. That is, it's the individual differences between people within age groups that matter most when predicting job performance.

The overall evidence indicates that age and job performance are unrelated.

What about factors such as cognitive abilities, absenteeism, turnover, and ability to learn? Studies comparing samples of older and younger workers in objective tests of cognitive abilities found no significant differences between the groups. Where small decreases in older workers have been found, it tends not to affect performance. Older workers appear to use their experience to cope and compensate for any age-related decline in cognitive skills.

The findings on absenteeism are mixed. While most studies show that absences decline with age, a closer examination finds it is partially a function of whether the absence is avoidable or unavoidable. In general, older employees have lower rates of avoidable absence than do younger employees. However, they have equal rates of unavoidable absence, such as those due to sickness.

In terms of turnover, the evidence is quite clear: The older you get, the less likely you are to quit your job. Of course, this isn't an unexpected finding. You would expect older workers to be more stable for several reasons. As workers get older, they have fewer alternative job opportunities because their skills have become more specialized. Additionally, their long tenure also often tends to provide them with higher wage rates, longer paid vacations, and more attractive pension benefits.

Finally, what about older workers' ability to learn? The evidence here is also mixed. Older workers can learn "new tricks," but often complete training more slowly than their younger counterparts. There is also evidence that the type of training may influence its effectiveness. Some training methods, such as active participation, modeling, and self-paced learning, appear to be more effective with older workers.

TRUTH

8

Match Personalities and Jobs

Want to increase the satisfaction of new employees and decrease the likelihood that they'll resign? There is a substantial amount of evidence that demonstrates this can be achieved by selecting job applicants whose personality matches the job you're trying to fill.

Six personality types have been identified, and evidence strongly supports that people are happiest when they are put in jobs that align with their personality. Those six personalities are realistic, investigative, social, conventional, enterprising, and artistic.

> People are happiest when they are put in jobs that align with their personality.

- **Realistic** people prefer physical activities that require skill, strength, and coordination. Their personality traits: shy, genuine, persistent, stable, conforming, and practical. Examples of jobs that align with their personality include mechanic, drill press operator, assembly-line worker, and farmer.

- **Investigative** people prefer activities that involve thinking, organizing, and understanding. Their personality traits: analytical, original, curious, and independent. Examples of jobs that align with their personality include biologist, economist, software programmer, mathematician, and news reporter.

- **Social** people prefer activities that involve helping and developing others. Their personality traits: sociable, friendly, cooperative, and understanding. Examples of jobs that align with their personality include social worker, teacher, counselor, and clinical psychologist.

- **Conventional** people prefer rule-regulated, orderly, and unambiguous activities. Their personality traits: conforming, efficient, practical, unimaginative, and inflexible. Examples of jobs that align with their personality include accountant, corporate manager, bank teller, and file clerk.

- **Enterprising** people prefer verbal activities in which there are opportunities to influence others and attain power. Their personality traits: self-confident, ambitious, energetic, and domineering. Examples of jobs that align with their personality include lawyer, real estate agent, public-relations specialist, and small-business manager.

- **Artistic** people prefer ambiguous and unsystematic activities that allow creative expression. Their personality traits: imaginative, disorderly, idealistic, emotional, and impractical. Examples of jobs that align with their personality include painter, musician, writer, and interior decorator.

The evidence indicates that people in jobs congruent with their personality tend to be more satisfied and less likely to voluntarily resign than people in incongruent jobs. Social individuals, for instance, should be in social jobs, conventional people in conventional jobs, and so forth. In addition, personalities can be conceptualized in a circle. Points on that circle would be in this order: realistic, investigative, artistic, social, enterprising, conventional, and back to realistic. Findings support that the closer two personalities are in that circle, the more compatible they are. And adjacent categories are most similar. So a realistic person in an investigative job is more congruent—and should be more content—than if he or she were in a social job.

Our conclusion is that managers should assess vocational interests in the hiring process. And when interests and job requirements are matched successfully, there is an increased likelihood that hires will perform well on the job and stay with the organization.

> Managers should assess vocational interests in the hiring process.

TRUTH

9

Hire People Who Fit Your Culture: My "Good Employee" Is Your Stinker!

Many a manager has hired a new employee based largely on his or her skills and then lived to regret it. While skill competence is certainly an important ingredient in the making of a "good employee," never underestimate the role that an organization's culture plays in an employee's success or failure.

Employee performance typically has a large subjective component. Bosses and colleagues have to make interpretations: Is Dave a team player? Is Tina taking unnecessary risks? Is Laura too competitive? And whether those interpretations are positive or negative depend to a great extent on how well an employee is perceived to fit into the organization. A good person-organization fit goes a long way toward ensuring that an employee will be perceived as a high performer.

> Never underestimate the role that an organization's culture plays in an employee's success or failure.

An organization's culture represents a system of shared meaning. It expresses the core values that are shared by a majority of the organization's members. The culture at Ireland's Ryanair, for example, values aggressiveness and competition. In contrast, Johnson & Johnson has a communal culture that emphasizes a strong family feel and values trust and loyalty. The typical "good" employee at Ryanair looks and behaves very differently from the typical "good" employee at J&J. Similarly, Walmart's obsession with cost-minimization creates a very different culture, and attracts and promotes a different type of employee than does Nordstrom, whose culture is defined by commitment to customer service.

As a manager, you should assess potential employees in terms of how well you think they will fit into your organization's culture. You want to hire people whose values are essentially consistent with those of the organization, or at least a good portion of those values. If you begin by getting a solid handle on what your organization values and rewards, you're well on your way to determining whether a candidate will be a good match. Ask questions and make observations that will allow you to determine the applicant's propensity to be innovative and take risks, to focus on "the big picture" versus the details, to emphasize means or ends, to be team oriented or individualistic, to be aggressive and competitive versus easygoing, and whether he or she prefers the status quo to growth. These are the primary elements that identify organizational cultures.

You should assess potential employees in terms of how well you think they will fit into your organization's culture.

What can you expect to happen if you make a mistake and hire a few candidates who don't fit with your firm's culture? It's likely you'll wind up with hires who lack motivation and commitment and who are dissatisfied with their jobs and the organization. They'll get lower performance evaluations than employees with similar objective performance but whose values align with the organization. And, not surprisingly, employee "misfits" have considerably higher turnover rates than individuals who perceive a good fit. Most people pick up the cues that they don't fit in and, assuming other job options are available, leave in search of a job where they're more likely to be appreciated.

TRUTH
9

HIRE PEOPLE WHO FIT YOUR CULTURE: MY "GOOD EMPLOYEE" IS YOUR STINKER!

TRUTH

10

Good Citizenship
Counts!

All other things equal, most managers want employees who will do more than their usual job duties. They want employees who will go beyond expectations. Employees who exhibit discretionary behavior that is not part of their formal job requirements, but that promotes the organization's operations, are said to be good citizens. And in today's workplace, where flexibility is critical, jobs are fluid, work is often done in teams, and job descriptions frequently fail to include all the essential tasks that need to be done, top-performing managers need individuals who display good citizenship behavior.

What *is* good citizenship behavior? Examples include employees making constructive statements about their work group and the organization, helping others on their team, volunteering for extra job activities, avoiding unnecessary conflicts, showing care for organizational property, respecting the spirit as well as the letter of rules and regulations, and gracefully tolerating the occasional work-related impositions and nuisances. Not surprisingly, studies indicate that those organizational units that have employees who exhibit good citizenship behaviors outperform those that don't.

Managers want employees who will go *beyond* expectations.

So what can managers do to stimulate good citizenship among employees? The answer seems to be: Treat people fairly. When people believe outcomes, treatment, and procedures are fair, they are more likely to talk positively about the organization, help others, and go beyond the normal expectations in their job. If your employees feel that you, your organization's procedures, and company pay policies are fair, trust is developed. And when employees trust you and the organization, they're more willing to voluntarily engage in behaviors that go beyond their formal job requirements.

Employees who exhibit good citizenship behaviors outperform those who don't.

11

Manage the Socialization of New Employees

All Marines must go through a multiweek boot camp, where they "prove" their commitment. At the same time, the Marine trainers are indoctrinating new recruits in the "Marine way." In a similar, but less elaborate manner, Starbucks puts all new employees through 24 hours of training to teach them the Starbucks philosophy, the company jargon, and the ins-and-outs of Starbucks' coffee business.

The Marines and Starbucks use their formal training programs to socialize new members. They're helping employees adapt to their organization's culture. Why? Because no matter how good a job an organization does in recruitment and selection, new employees are not fully indoctrinated in the organization's culture. Socialization turns outsiders into insiders and fine-tunes employee behaviors so they align with what management wants.

> Socialization turns outsiders into insiders and fine-tunes employee behaviors so they align with what management wants.

When hiring a new employee, you have four decisions you can make— each of which will affect the shaping of that new hires' behavior:

First, *will socialization be formal or informal?* The more a new employee is segregated from the ongoing work setting and differentiated in some way to make explicit his or her newcomer's role, the more formal socialization is. The Marines and Starbucks' specific orientation and training programs are examples of a formal process. Informal socialization just puts the new employee directly into his or her job, with little or no special attention.

Second, *will socialization be done individually or collectively?* Most employees are socialized individually. But they also can be grouped together and processed through an identical set of experiences as in military boot camp.

Third, *will socialization be serial or random?* Serial socialization is characterized by the use of role models who train and encourage the newcomer. Apprenticeship and mentoring programs are examples. In random socialization, role models are deliberately withheld. The new employee is left on his or her own to figure things out.

Finally, *will socialization seek investiture or divestiture?* Investiture assumes that the newcomer's qualities and qualifications are the necessary ingredients for job success, so these qualities and qualifications are confirmed and supported. Divestiture tries to strip away certain characteristics of the new hire. College fraternity and sorority "pledges" go through divestiture socialization to shape them into the proper role.

Generally speaking, the more that management relies on socialization programs that are formal, collective, serial, and emphasize divestiture, the greater the likelihood that newcomers' differences and perspectives will be stripped away and replaced by standardized and predictable behaviors. Conversely, the use of informal, individual, random, and investiture options will create a workforce of individualists. So managers can use socialization as

Managers can use socialization as a tool.

a tool to create conformists who maintain traditions and customs or, at the other extreme, inventive and creative individuals who consider no organizational practice sacred.

TRUTH

12

Why Many Workers Aren't Motivated at Work Today

I often hear experienced managers complain that "people just aren't motivated to work anymore." If this is true, the fault is with managers and organizational practices, not the employees! When employees lack motivation, the problem almost always lies in one of five areas: selection, ambiguous goals, the performance appraisal system, the organization's reward system, or in the manager's inability to shape employee's perception of the appraisal and reward systems.

The best way to understand employee motivation is to think of it as being dependent on three relationships. When all three of these relationships are strong, employees tend to be motivated. If any one or more of these relationships are weak, employee effort is likely to suffer. I'll present these relationships in terms of questions.

> If employees aren't motivated, the fault is with managers and organizational practices, not the employees!

First, do employees believe that if they give a maximum effort, it will be recognized in their performance appraisal? For a lot of employees, the answer is unfortunately: No. Why? Their skill level may be deficient, which means that no matter how hard they try, they're not likely to be high performers. Or, if the organization's performance appraisal system is designed to assess nonperformance factors such as loyalty or initiative, more effort won't necessarily result in a higher appraisal. Still another possibility is that the employee, rightly or wrongly, perceives that he or she is disliked by the boss. As a result, the employee will expect to get a poor appraisal regardless of his or her level of effort. These examples suggest that one possible source of low employee motivation is the employee's belief that, no matter how hard he or she works, the likelihood of getting a good performance appraisal is low.

Second, do employees believe that if they get a good performance appraisal, it will lead to organizational rewards? Many employees see the performance-reward relationship in their job as weak. The reason is that organizations reward a lot of things besides just performance. For example, when

Many employees see the performance-reward relationship in their job as weak.

pay is allocated to employees on the basis of seniority or "kissing up" to the boss, employees are likely to see the performance-reward relationship as being weak and demotivating.

Last, are the rewards the employees receive the ones that they want? An employee may work hard in hopes of getting a promotion, but gets a pay raise instead. Or an employee wants a more interesting and challenging job, but receives only a few words of praise. Or an employee puts in extra effort, expecting to be relocated to the company's Paris office, but instead is transferred to Phoenix. These examples illustrate the importance of tailoring the rewards to individual employee needs. Sadly, many managers are limited in the rewards they can distribute, so it's difficult for them to individualize rewards. Moreover, some managers incorrectly assume that all employees want the same thing and overlook the motivational effects of differentiating rewards. In either case, employee motivation is suboptimized.

In summary, a lot of employees lack motivation at work because they see a weak relationship between their effort and performance, between performance and organizational rewards, and/or between the rewards they receive and the ones they really want. If you want motivated employees, you need to do what's necessary to strengthen these relationships.

TRUTH

13

Telling Employees to "Do Your Best" Isn't Likely to Achieve Their Best

A friend of mine, who manages a group of software programmers in Seattle, was recently telling me what a great staff he had and how much faith he had in them. "When I hand out an assignment, I merely tell my people, 'Do your best. No one can ask more of you than that.'" I think my friend was a bit perplexed when I told him that wasn't the best way to motivate his staff. I felt pretty confident in telling him that he would have better success by giving specific and challenging goals to each employee or work team.

There is a mountain of evidence that tells us that people perform best when they have goals. More to the point, we can say that specific goals increase performance; that difficult goals, when accepted, result in higher performance than do easy goals; and that feedback leads to higher performance than does nonfeedback.

Specific hard goals produce a higher level of output than does the generalized goal of "do your best." Why? It's the specificity of the goal itself that acts as an internal stimulus. Goals tell employees what needs to be done and how much effort they'll need to expend to achieve it. For instance, if my Seattle friend's software programmers committed to complete their current project by the last business day of next month, they would now have a specific objective to try to attain. We can say that, all things being equal, the individual or team with a specific goal will outperform his or her counterparts operating with no goals or the generalized goal of "do your best."

If factors such as ability and acceptance of the goals are held constant, we can also state with confidence that the more difficult the goal, the higher the level of performance. More difficult goals encourage people to extend their reach and work harder. Of course, it's logical to assume that easier goals are more likely to be accepted. But once an employee accepts a hard task, he or she is likely to exert

> Specific hard goals produce a higher level of output than does the generalized goal of "do your best."

a high level of effort to achieve it. The challenge for managers is to have employees see difficult goals as attainable.

There is considerable evidence that tells us that people will do better when they get feedback on how well they're progressing toward their goals because feedback helps to identify discrepancies between what they've accomplished and what they want to do. That is, feedback acts to guide behavior. But all feedback is not equally potent. Self-generated feedback—in which an employee is able to monitor his or her own progress—has been shown to be a more powerful motivator than externally generated feedback from a boss or coworkers.

The advice given here about specific hard goals and feedback may seem obvious or even trite. But, in practice, a large number of managers continue to ignore their value. Studies consistently show a large percentage of employees believe they lack specific goals on their job and also complain about a lack of performance feedback.

A large percentage of employees believe they lack specific goals on their job.

One final point before we leave this topic: Our claims about the power of goals is culture bound. Goals are well adapted to countries such as the United States and Canada because they mesh well with North American cultures. Goals require employees to be reasonably independent and employers to put a high importance on performance. Those requirements are not necessarily true in every country. For instance, don't expect goals to necessarily lead to higher employee performance in countries such as Portugal or Chile.

TRUTH

14

Not Everyone Wants to Participate in Setting Goals

Contemporary managers have been well schooled in the importance of using participation—that is, having managers share a significant degree of decision-making power with their employees. Participative leadership and decision making have been preached by business schools since the 1960s. For instance, the late management-guru Peter Drucker considered participation in goal setting to be a necessary part of his Management By Objectives doctrine. Some academics have even proposed that participative management is an ethical imperative.

In the last 50-plus years, we have seen the decline (and near extinction) of the autocrat, to be replaced by the participative manager. So you might find it surprising that when it comes to setting goals, we discover an interesting finding: It may not matter if employee goals are assigned by the boss or participatively set. The evidence shows little consistent superiority for goals that are set participatively between employees and their bosses over those unilaterally assigned by bosses.

The logic behind participation is well known. As jobs have become more complex, managers rarely know everything their employees do. Thus, participation allows those who know the most to contribute. Participation also increases commitment to decisions. People are less likely to undermine a decision at the time of its implementation if they shared in making that decision. But the evidence doesn't support the idea that participatively set goals are superior to assigned ones. In some cases, participatively set goals achieve superior performance; in other cases, individuals perform best when assigned goals by their boss. The only advantage that participation may provide is that it tends to increase acceptance of a goal. People are more likely to accept even a difficult goal if it is participatively set rather than arbitrarily assigned by their boss. Thus, although participative goals may have no superiority over assigned goals when acceptance is taken as a given, participation does increase the probability that more difficult goals will be agreed to and acted upon.

> The evidence doesn't support the idea that participatively set goals are superior to assigned ones.

You may be wondering: Why wouldn't people always do better under participatively set goals? That's a good question. Let me attempt an answer. The explanation may lie in the conditions that are required for participation to be effective. For participation to work, there must be adequate time to participate, the issues in which employees get involved must be relevant to their interests, employees must have the ability (intelligence, technical knowledge, communication skills) to participate, and the organization's culture must support employee involvement. These conditions are not always met in many work places. In addition, while behavioral scientists often ignore this reality, the truth is that some people don't want the responsibilities that come with participation. They prefer to be told what to do and let their boss do the worrying. These conditions and realities may explain why the use of employee participation is no sure means for improving employee performance.

> Participation is no sure means for improving employee performance.

TRUTH

15

Professional Workers Go for the Flow

Can you think of times in your life when you've been so deeply involved in something that nothing else seems to matter? The task consumes you totally and you lose track of time. Most people can. It's most likely to occur when you're doing a favorite activity: running, skiing, dancing, reading a novel, playing a computer game, listening to music, cooking an elegant meal. This totally involved state is called flow. Managers should look to flow as a particularly effective way to motivate professional employees.

Research finds that the flow experience itself isn't necessarily a time when people are happy. It's a period of deep concentration. But when a flow task is completed, and the individual looks back on what has happened, he or she is flooded with feelings of gratitude for the experience. It's then that the person realizes the satisfaction received from the experience and how it made him or her happier.

> The flow experience isn't necessarily a time when people are happy.

Are there conditions that are likely to produce flow? Yes. When people describe flow experiences, they talk about common characteristics in the tasks they were doing. The tasks were challenging and required using a high level of skills. The tasks were goal-directed and provided them with feedback on how well they were performing. The tasks also demanded total concentration and creativity. And the tasks were so consuming that people had no attention left over to think about anything irrelevant or to worry about problems.

Here's something that might surprise you: The flow experience is rarely reported by people when they're doing leisure activities such as watching television or relaxing. Flow is *most likely* to be experienced *at work*, not at home!

If you ask people whether they'd like to work less, the answer is almost always yes. People associate leisure with happiness. They think if they had more free time, they'd be happier. Studies of thousands of individuals suggest that people are generally wrong in this belief.

Flow is *most likely* to be experienced *at work*, not at home.

When people spend time at home, for instance, they often lack a clear purpose, don't know how well they're doing, get distracted, and feel that their skills are underutilized. They frequently describe themselves as bored. But work has many of the properties that stimulate flow. It often has clear goals. It provides people with feedback on how well they're doing—either from the work process itself or through a boss's evaluation. People's skills are typically matched to their jobs, which provides challenge. And jobs usually encourage concentration and prevent distractions. The end result is that work, rather than leisure, more clearly mirrors the flow that people might get from games, sport, music, or art.

What are the managerial implications from flow research? Work, itself, can be a powerful motivator. It can provide a feeling of happiness that most leisure activities can't. So, where possible, design jobs with challenging, creative, and consuming tasks that allow employees to utilize their skills, and ensure that these tasks have clear goals and provide employees with feedback.

TRUTH

16

When Giving Feedback: Criticize Behaviors, Not People

It seems pretty simple, but it's amazing how many managers ignore this advice when giving feedback to employees: Criticize employee behaviors, not the people themselves. Successful feedback focuses on specific behavior and is impersonal.

Feedback should be specific rather than general. Managers should avoid making statements such as "You have a bad attitude" or "I'm really impressed with the good job you did." These types of statements are vague and, while they provide information, they don't tell the employee enough to correct the "bad attitude" or on *what basis* it

> Successful feedback focuses on specific behavior and is impersonal.

was concluded that a "good job" had been done. For clarity, here are some examples of what good feedback is like: "Bob, I'm concerned with your attitude toward your work. You were a half-hour late to yesterday's staff meeting, and then you told me you hadn't read the preliminary report we were discussing. Today, you tell me you're taking off three hours early for a dental appointment"; or "Jan, I was really pleased with the job you did on the Phillips account. They increased their purchases from us by 22 percent last month, and I got a call a few days ago from Dan Phillips complimenting me on how quickly you responded to those specification changes for the MJ-7 microchip." Both of these statements focus on specific behaviors. They tell the recipient *why* you are being critical or complimentary.

In addition, feedback—especially the negative kind—should be descriptive rather than judgmental or evaluative. No matter how upset a manager might be, for instance, he or she should keep the feedback job-related and never criticize someone personally because of an inappropriate action. Telling people they're "stupid," "incompetent," or the like is almost always counterproductive. It provokes such an emotional reaction that the performance deviation itself is apt to be overlooked. When a manager is criticizing an employee, that manager is censuring a job-related behavior, not the person. You may be tempted to tell someone he or she is "rude and insensitive" (which may be true); however, that's hardly impersonal. Better to say something like, "You interrupted me three times with questions that were not urgent, when you knew I was talking long distance to a customer in Ireland."

Feedback should be descriptive rather than judgmental or evaluative.

One final point on feedback: If negative, make sure the behavior is controllable by the recipient. There's little constructive value in reminding a person of some shortcoming over which he or she has no control. Negative feedback, therefore, should be directed toward behavior the recipient can do something about. So, for example, to criticize an employee who is late because he forgot to set his wake-up alarm is valid. To criticize him for being late when the subway he takes to work every day had a power failure, trapping him underground for half an hour, is pointless. There is nothing he could do to correct what happened.

17

Managing Across the
Generation Gap

Jan Stewart couldn't believe her ears. On her phone was the mother of one of her employees, complaining about the long hours that Ms. Stewart was asking her son to put in at work. Said Stewart, "I've had employees complain to me before, but never a parent!"

Jan Stewart was getting a first-hand taste of what it can be like managing employees who have been coddled and protected by "helicopter" parents. Welcome to the challenges of managing workers from Generation Y.

Most current employees fall into one of three generational groups, differentiated by when they were born. There are the Baby Boomers, born between 1946 and 1964; the Gen Xers, born between 1965 and 1977; and Generation Y, also sometimes referred to as the Net Generation or Millennials. They were born between 1978 and 1991. Does the fact that two employees were both born in the same year mean that they will definitely have a set of common values? No. But values are imprinted for life by defining historical events. Shared experiences then lead to shaping common values. So the following insights can help you to better understand individual values and mindsets, the differences between generations, and the challenges of managing and motivating workers born in different eras.

Values are imprinted for life by defining historical events.

Baby Boomers were born after World War II when veterans returned to their families. Growing up in the 1950s and 1960s, Boomers were influenced by times of prosperity, safety, and the belief that anything is possible. And being the largest generation in history, they are inherently competitive. They entered the workforce from the mid-1960s through the mid-1980s. They place a great deal of emphasis on achievement and material success, but dislike authoritarianism and laziness. Managers should give these employees challenging goals and leave them alone.

The lives of Gen Xers have been shaped by globalization, two-career parents, MTV, AIDS, and computers. Xers value flexibility, life options, and the achievement of job satisfaction. As the children of workaholic Baby Boomers, they grew up as latchkey kids. They tend to be independent and self-reliant. Family and relationships are very important. In search of balance in their lives, Xers are less willing to make personal sacrifices for the sake of their employer. They strive for work-life balance. So managers should give these employees flexibility and provide them with the freedom to balance work and personal obligations.

Generation Y has been shaped by helicopter parents who hovered over their children and focused on building self-esteem. These parents downplayed competition and believed that there should be no winners and losers—everyone gets a participatory ribbon! Gen Y prefers teamwork, continuous performance feedback, and is totally at ease with technology. They are good at multitasking and have a strong desire to learn new things. They are also ambitious, but often unrealistic, in their career expectations; and often characterized as entitled and needy. They want bosses who provide ongoing coaching or mentoring and give preference to a good workplace over salary or benefits. Managers

> Gen Y prefers teamwork, continuous performance feedback, and is totally at ease with technology.

should give Gen Y regular feedback, provide clear guidance, design work around team collaboration, and widen job descriptions to allow opportunities to learn new skills.

TRUTH

18

You Get What You Reward

A management consultant specializing in police research noticed that, in one community, officers would come on duty for their shift, proceed to get into their police cars, drive to the highway that cut through the town, and speed back and forth along this highway for their entire shift. Clearly, this fast cruising had little to do with good police work. But this behavior made considerably more sense once the consultant learned that the community's city council used mileage on police vehicles as a measure of police effectiveness. The city council unintentionally was rewarding "putting lots of miles on police cars," so that's what officers emphasized.

Managers routinely reward employee behaviors they're trying to discourage and fail to reward the behaviors they actually want. A few examples illustrate this sad fact: Management says it wants to build teamwork, actually rewards individual accomplishments, and then wonders why employees compete against each other and are constantly looking out for Number One. Management talks up the importance of quality but then ignores employees who turn out shoddy work and punishes those who fail to meet their production goals because they're focusing on quality. Senior executives speak out loudly about the importance of their managers acting ethically and then give a big promotion to a manager whose ethical conduct is clearly suspect.

Consistent with Truth 12, Why Many Workers Aren't Motivated at Work Today," managers who claim that their employees seem to be lacking motivation should review their reward systems to consider the possibility that they're paying off for behavior other than what they're seeking. This review should begin by assessing what types of behaviors are currently being rewarded. What this assessment too often finds is that organizations are not rewarding what they assume they are. Obviously, if this is the case,

> Managers routinely reward employee behaviors they're trying to discourage and fail to reward the behaviors they actually want.

then the reward system needs to be changed to get the desired behaviors. If you want quality, reward quality. If you want ethical behavior, then reward employees who act ethically.

If you want quality, reward quality.

Modifying reward systems doesn't have to be a complex undertaking. Small adjustments can make big differences. And the little techniques you use at home can often be applied at the workplace. For instance, if you buy a single candy bar for your two kids, can you expect them to fight over who gets which half? Probably. Have you ever just given the candy bar to one of them, told him to cut it in half, and then let his brother or sister have first choice on which half he or she wants? This simple process of rewarding joint responsibility typically results in a precise and fair slicing up of the candy bar and a marked decline in fighting. This same logic was recently used by a department head who had to allocate offices in the company's new building. Two of his employees, who had never gotten along, were wasting a lot of time arguing which one of the 10 offices allocated to the department each would take. It seemed that whichever one Dave wanted, that would also be the one that Chuck preferred. After weeks of haggling, the department head told Dave to make two choices and that he was going to let Chuck make the first selection and Dave would get the other. The end result was that Dave sought two offices that were both acceptable to him, Chuck got "the pick of the litter," and both were happy.

One last comment. The importance of rewarding the right behaviors never was clearer to me than when I saw a rich relative continually tell her son, "Don't worry about saving money. You'll have plenty when I'm gone." That relative lived a very long life, and she could never understand why her son looked forward to her demise. Clearly, she would have gotten a very different behavior from her son had she made his inheritance conditioned on her longevity. He would have been far more supportive of her living a long life had she said in her latter years, "I'm going to give you $50,000 the first of every year for as long as I live. But when I go, all my remaining money will go to charity." Had she taken this approach, her son would have a vested interest in prolonging her life, not shortening it!

TRUTH

19

It's All Relative!

A quarterback in the National Football League tells his team's management that he won't be reporting to training camp. Although he's under contract and scheduled to make $9.5 million this season, he says he's not motivated to play this year. He wants his team to either renegotiate his contract or trade him so he can get more money. Neither this player nor his agent ever suggests that $9.5 million is inadequate to live on. The argument is almost always couched in terms of relative rewards: "Other players who aren't as good as I am [haven't played as long; haven't won as many awards; don't have as impressive statistics] are earning more."

There is an impressive body of evidence that tells us that employees don't look only at absolute rewards. They look at relative rewards. They compare what inputs they bring to a job (in terms of experience, effort, education, and competence) with the outcomes they receive (salary levels, pay raises, recognition, and the like). Then they look around for other references to compare themselves against. Those other references may be friends, relatives, neighbors, coworkers, colleagues in other organizations, or past jobs they have had. Finally, they compare their input/outcome ratio with the others and assess how equitably they think they're being treated. For our football player, he looks at his pay and his statistics; compares them with similar professional players at his position; and cries "foul" because he thinks he's under-rewarded.

> An impressive body of evidence tells us that employees don't look only at absolute rewards; they look at relative rewards.

When people make these comparisons, they come to one of three conclusions: They're either being *fairly treated, under-rewarded,* or *over-rewarded.* Fair treatment has a positive effect on motivation. Employees are likely to be motivated when they feel they are being equitably rewarded for their contribution.

However, when people perceive themselves as being under-rewarded, they tend to get angry. To lessen this anger and restore equity, they are likely to engage in behavioral or perceptual adjustments. For instance, they might take more paid sick leave, come in late to work or leave early, take longer breaks, put out less effort, goof-off on company time, ask for a raise, or even steal from the company in an attempt to "get what's mine." They might also reassess either their own or others' inputs and outcomes, or change the person or persons with whom they're comparing themselves. At the extreme, under-rewarded employees can become angry enough to quit. The degree of active behavior that under-rewarded employees will take is largely dependent on how equity-sensitive they are. Some employees are very good at ignoring inequities or adjusting their perceptions to make them less bothersome. But many professional and technical employees are quite equity-sensitive. They're likely to move quickly to correct any perceived inequity.

> People seem to have a great deal more tolerance of overpayment inequities than underpayment, or they're better able to rationalize them.

When people perceive themselves as over-rewarded, they react with guilt. And to relieve that guilt, they might work harder, get more education, help out others, or work through a paid vacation. Not surprisingly, the guilt rarely leads to requests for reductions in pay. In fact, people seem to have a great deal more tolerance of overpayment inequities than underpayment, or they're better able to rationalize them.

TRUTH

20

Recognition Motivates (and It Costs Very Little)

A few years back, 1,500 employees in a variety of work settings were surveyed to find out what they considered to be the most powerful workplace motivator. Their response? Recognition, recognition, and more recognition! Another study found that employees rated personal thanks from a manager for a job well done as the most motivating of a variety of incentives offered. But, unfortunately, 58 percent of the workers in this study said their managers didn't typically give such thanks.

In today's highly competitive global economy, most organizations are under severe cost pressures. That makes recognition programs particularly attractive. Why? In contrast to most other motivators, recognizing an employee's superior performance often costs little or no money. Maybe that's why a recent survey found that 80 percent of large companies have recognition programs. Popular recognition actions, beyond verbal and written acknowledgments, include merchandise, gift cards, and travel. Recognition has been found to be especially relevant in the motivation of low-wage workers. It costs little and helps to build employee self-esteem. For instance, Fine Host Corp., a food service firm in Connecticut, gives out quality awards and posts workers names in company buildings to recognize good work. All Metro Health Care in Lynbrook, New York, sponsors an award for home health care giver of the year and also gives employees gifts, such as watches and blenders, for scoring high in quarterly training exercises.

The most powerful workplace motivator is recognition, recognition, and more recognition!

We have a wealth of evidence that tells us that rewarding a behavior with recognition immediately following that behavior is likely to encourage its repetition. How can managers use this to help motivate employees? They can personally congratulate an employee in private for a good job. They can send a handwritten note or an e-mail message acknowledging something positive that the employee has done. For employees with a strong need for social acceptance, managers can publicly recognize accomplishments.

And to enhance group cohesiveness and motivation, managers can celebrate team successes. They can use meetings to recognize the contributions and achievements of successful work teams.

And keep in mind, little things can mean a lot. Lee Memorial Health System, in Cape Coral, Florida, found this out when it gave customized key chains to each of its 5,000 employees as a "thank you" when *Modern Healthcare* magazine named Lee as one of the top integrated health care networks in the United States. The key chains, designed especially for Lee Memorial, had the words "Valued Employee Since" displayed on the top of the brass emblem and the employee's year of hire added below. They cost Lee only $4.50 per employee, but they proved to be a powerful motivator. Lee's CEO said, "In all my years in health care administration, I've never witnessed as much excitement as was created by giving the key chains to our staff. I received many thank you notes and e-mails expressing appreciation that we would take the time to recognize each employee individually.

One caveat for any recognition effort: The recognition must be sincere. People can see through insincerity. So, for example, giving praise for a performance that is not out of the ordinary is likely to have little motivating potential.

Rewarding a behavior with recognition immediately following that behavior is likely to encourage its repetition.

RECOGNITION MOTIVATES (AND IT COSTS VERY LITTLE)

TRUTH
21

There's More to High
Employee Performance
Than Just Motivation

Robin and Chris both graduated from college a couple of years ago with degrees in elementary education. They each took jobs as first grade teachers but in different school districts. Robin immediately confronted a number of obstacles on the job: a large class (38 students), a small and dingy classroom, and inadequate supplies. Chris's situation couldn't have been more different. He had only 15 students in his class, plus a teaching aid for 15 hours each week, a modern and well-lighted room, a well-stocked supply cabinet, a computer for each student, and a highly supportive principal. Not surprisingly, at the end of the first school year, Chris had been considerably more effective as a teacher than had Robin.

The preceding episode illustrates an obvious but often overlooked fact: Success on a job is facilitated or hindered by the existence or absence of support resources. No matter how motivated an employee is, his or her performance is going to suffer if there isn't a supportive work environment.

A popular way of thinking about employee performance is as a function of the interaction of ability and motivation; that is, performance = $f(A \times M)$. If either ability or motivation is inadequate, performance will be negatively affected. This helps to explain, for instance, the hardworking athlete with modest abilities who consistently outperforms his or her more gifted, but lazy, rivals. But an important piece of the performance puzzle is still missing. We need to add opportunity to our equation. Performance = $f(A \times M \times O)$. Even though an individual may be willing and able, there may be obstacles that constrain performance.

> No matter how motivated an employee is, his or her performance is going to suffer if there isn't a supportive work environment.

When you attempt to assess why an employee may not be performing to the level that you believe he or she is capable of, take a look at the work environment to see if it's supportive. Does the employee have adequate tools, equipment, materials, and supplies? Does the employee have favorable working conditions, helpful coworkers, supportive work rules and procedures, sufficient information to make job-related decisions, adequate time to do a good job, and the like? If not, performance will suffer. And don't forget to minimize your employees' disruptions and distractions. As we'll discuss in Truth 39, "Watch Out for Digital Distractions," today's workers are particularly vulnerable to a wide range of digital distractions—from tweets to Facebook to Internet videos.

TRUTH

22

Five Leadership Myths Debunked

With the possible exception of wrinkle removers and weight-loss programs, there may be no subject with more nonsense masquerading as truth than the topic of leadership. Let's look at five popular leadership myths.

Myth #1. Leaders are born, not made. A prominent myth is that leadership qualities are inherent in the individual: A select group of people are born to lead, while most of us are born to follow. The evidence indicates that genetics does have some influence on leadership emergence. Studies indicate that about 30 percent of leadership emergence can be accounted for by genetic factors. But that still leaves 70 percent to environmental influences. So while a few traits associated with leadership are genetically determined, leadership can be learned. We are not prisoners of our genetic makeup when it comes to whether or not we choose to seek leadership positions.

Myth #2. Successful leaders have common traits. The media are particularly guilty here of looking for and promoting a common set of characteristics they think leaders have. They identify leaders such as Richard Branson, the late Steve Jobs, and Barack Obama in terms such as *charismatic*, *enthusiastic*, *decisive*, and *courageous*. What does the evidence reveal? A number of traits seem to regularly appear that differentiate leaders from others. They include ambition and energy, the desire to lead, self-confidence, and intelligence. Overall, it appears that these traits are relatively powerful at explaining people's perceptions of leadership. However, you shouldn't put much faith in the belief that successful leaders have common traits. Why? First, traits provide no guarantees. Rather than being applicable across *all* situations, they appear to predict leadership in *selective* situations. Second, the evidence is unclear in separating cause from effect. For example, are leaders self-confident, or does success as a leader build self-confidence? And finally, traits do a better job at predicting the *appearance* of leadership than in actually distinguishing between effective and ineffective leaders. We can't say that possessing traits like ambition and self-confidence will predict effective leaders, merely that others are likely to perceive them as such.

Myth #3. Men make better leaders than women. Leadership positions have historically been held by men. As such, perceptions of leadership are often characterized in masculine terms such as strong, aggressive, and assertive. The evidence, however, indicates that men have no advantage over women when it comes to leadership. Since men historically held the great majority of leadership positions, a stereotype developed of leaders that had a masculine bias— task-oriented, directive, unemotional. But as organizations have increasingly become structured around flexibility, teamwork, trust, and information sharing, the male stereotype of a directive leader has become far less pervasive. Organizations increasingly need fewer leaders who use a command-and-control style and more who encourage participation, share power and information, nurture their followers, and lead through inclusion. The most recent evidence suggests that, although the differences are small, if one gender does have an advantage, it's probably women.

Myth #4. The MBA creates effective leaders. Master's degrees in business administration are popular and expensive. The U.S., alone, is turning out more than 155,000 MBAs every year. And the price of an MBA is not trivial. The cost of an MBA at a top university now exceeds $100,000. For many fast-trackers, pursuing an MBA also means giving up a full-time job and, typically, an income of $150,000 or more during that two-year period. Given these facts, you'd think there would be substantial evidence that MBA programs are successful in creating leaders. The evidence says otherwise. Little of what goes on in the conventional MBA program helps build effective leadership skills. These programs are great for learning about business, but they don't train leaders. While they talk a lot about the importance of leadership, actual leadership is learned through experience and practice. And these are areas where MBA programs come up short. As one noted authority put it, "the MBA trains the wrong people, in the wrong ways."

> Little of what goes on in the conventional MBA program helps build effective leadership skills.

Myth #5. Leadership always matters. Given all the attention leadership receives—in business schools, politics, the media—you'd think leadership was always necessary for a group or organization (or country) to be successful. It isn't. Data from numerous studies collectively demonstrate that, in many situations, whatever actions leaders take are irrelevant. Why? There are individual, job, and organizational factors that limit the influence of a leader on his or her subordinates. Characteristics of subordinates such as their experience, training, or indifference toward organizational rewards can substitute for the effect of leaders. Experience and training, for example, can replace the need for a leader's support or ability to clarify work tasks. Jobs that are inherently unambiguous and routine or that are intrinsically satisfying may require little direct attention from formal leaders. And organizational characteristics such as explicit formalized goals, rigid rules and procedures, or cohesive work groups can minimize the role of formal leaders.

> In many situations, whatever actions leaders take are irrelevant.

TRUTH
23

The Essence of Leadership Is Trust

When we trust others, we assume they'll act honestly and truthfully, and be reliable and predictable. We also assume they won't take advantage of our trust. Trust is the essence of leadership because it's impossible to lead people who don't trust you.

One author summarized the link between trust and leadership this way: "Part of the leader's task has been, and continues to be, working with people to find and solve problems, but whether leaders gain access to the knowledge and creative thinking they need to solve problems depends on how much people trust them. Trust and trustworthiness modulate the leader's access to knowledge and cooperation."

> It's impossible to lead people who don't trust you.

When employees trust a leader, they're willing to be vulnerable to the leader's actions—confident that their rights and interests won't be abused. People are unlikely to look up to or follow someone whom they perceive as dishonest or who is likely to take advantage of them. Honesty, for instance, consistently ranks at the top of most people's list of characteristics they admire in their leaders. It's an absolutely essential component of leadership.

Now, maybe more than any time in the past, managerial and leadership effectiveness depends on the ability to gain the trust of followers. Why? Because in times of change and instability—which characterizes most workplaces today—people turn to personal relationships for guidance, and the quality of these relationships is largely determined by the level of trust. In addition, contemporary management practices such as empowerment and the use of work teams require trust to be effective.

> Honesty consistently ranks at the top of most people's list of characteristics they admire in their leaders.

So how do you, as a manager, get employees to trust you? It's no simple task, but there are actions that research indicates help to build trusting relationships:

- **Be open.** Mistrust comes as much from what people don't know as from what they do know. Keep people informed, make the criteria on how decisions are made overtly clear, explain the rationale for your decisions, be candid about problems, and fully disclose relevant information.

- **Be fair.** Before making decisions or taking actions, consider how others will perceive them in terms of objectivity and fairness. Give credit where it's due, be objective and impartial in performance appraisals, and pay attention to equity perceptions in reward distributions.

- **Speak your feelings.** Managers who convey only hard facts come across as cold and distant. If you share your feelings, others will see you as real and human.

- **Tell the truth.** Truth is an inherent part of integrity. Once you have lied and been found out, your ability to gain and hold trust is largely diminished. People are generally more tolerant of learning something they "don't want to hear" than finding out that their manager lied to them.

- **Show consistency.** People want predictability. Mistrust comes from not knowing what to expect. Let your central values and beliefs guide your actions. This increases consistency and builds trust.

- **Fulfill your promises.** Trust requires that people believe that you are dependable. So you need to ensure that you keep your word and commitments.

- **Maintain confidences.** People trust those who are discreet and upon whom they can rely. They need to feel assured that you will not discuss their confidences with others or betray that confidence. If people perceive you as someone who leaks personal confidences or someone who can't be depended on, you won't be perceived as trustworthy.

TRUTH

24

Experience Counts! Wrong!

Most of us accept the commonsense notion that experience is a valuable, even necessary, component for effective leadership. Voters, for instance, tend to believe that the jobs of U.S. senator or state governor prepare individuals to be effective U.S. presidents. Similarly, organizations buy into this notion when they carefully screen outside candidates for senior management positions on the basis of their experience. For that matter, have you ever filled out an employment application that didn't ask about previous experience or job history? In many instances, experience is used as the single most important factor in hiring and promotion decisions. Well, here's the surprising news: The evidence doesn't support that experience per se contributes to leadership effectiveness.

"Some inexperienced leaders have been outstandingly successful, while many experienced leaders have been outstanding failures. Among the most highly regarded former presidents are Abraham Lincoln and Harry Truman, who had very little previous leadership, while highly experienced Herbert Hoover and Franklin Pierce were among the least successful." Studies of military officers, research and development teams, shop supervisors, post office administrators, and school principals tell us that experienced managers tend to be no more effective than the managers with little experience.

> Have you ever filled out an employment application that *didn't* ask about previous experience?

How could it be that experience wouldn't make leaders more effective? Intuitively, it would seem that experience would provide learning opportunities that would translate into improved on-the-job leadership skills. The problems seem to be twofold. First, quality of experience and time in the job are not necessarily the same thing. Second, there is variability between situations that influence the transferability of experience.

One flaw in the "experience counts" logic is the assumption that length of time on a job is actually a measure of experience. This says nothing about the quality of experience. The fact that one person has 20 years' experience while another has 2 years' experience doesn't necessarily mean that the former has had 10 times as many meaningful experiences. Too often, 20 years of experience is nothing other than 1 year of experience repeated 20 times! In even the most complex jobs, real learning typically ends after 2 or 3 years. By then, almost all new and unique situations have been experienced. So one problem with trying to link experience with leadership effectiveness is not paying attention to the quality and diversity of the experience.

The second problem is the situations in which experience is obtained are rarely comparable to new situations. It's critical to take into consideration the relevance of past experience to a new situation. Jobs differ, support resources differ, organizational cultures differ, follower characteristics differ, and so on. A primary reason that leadership experience isn't strongly related to leadership performance is undoubtedly due to variability of situations.

> Too often, 20 years of experience is nothing other than 1 year of experience repeated 20 times!

So what can we conclude? When selecting people for leadership positions, be careful not to place too much emphasis on their experience. Experience, per se, is not a very good predictor of effectiveness. Just because a candidate has 10 years of previous leadership experience is no assurance that his or her experience will transfer to a new situation. What is relevant is the quality of previous experience and the relevance of that experience to the new situation that the leader will face.

25

Effective Leaders Know How to Frame Issues

Martin Luther King, Jr.'s "I Have a Dream" speech largely shaped the civil rights movement. His words created an image of what a country would be like where racial prejudice no longer existed; that is, King framed the civil rights movement in a way so others would see it the way he saw it.

Framing is a way to use language to manage meaning. It involves the selection and highlighting of one or more aspects of a subject while excluding others.

Framing is analogous to what a photographer does. The visual world that exists is essentially ambiguous. When a photographer aims her camera and focuses on a specific shot, she frames her photo. Others then see what she wanted them to see. That is precisely what leaders do when they frame an issue. They choose which aspects or portion of the subject they want others to focus on and which portions they want to be excluded.

> Framing is a way to use language to manage meaning.

Political leaders live or die on their ability to frame problems and their opponent's image. In an age of language wars, political victory often goes to those who win the battle over terminology. For instance, in recent years, few topics have generated as much "framing" in Washington as what defines a *fair tax*. Democrats argue that it is one that is steeply progressive and puts most of the weight on the wealthy. Republicans counter that a fair tax is one that spreads the tax burden more evenly and requires everyone to pay.

> Political leaders live or die on their ability to frame problems and their opponent's image.

In the complex and chaotic environment in which most leaders work, there is typically considerable maneuverability with respect to "the facts." What is real is often what the leader says is real.

Framing influences leadership effectiveness in numerous ways. It largely shapes the decision process in that frames determine the problems that need attention, the causes attributed to the problems, and the eventual choices for solving the problems. Framing also increases a leader's success in implementing goals and getting people's agreement, because once the right frames are in place, the right behavior follows. In addition, framing is critical to effective leadership in a global context because leaders must frame problems in common ways to prevent cultural misunderstandings. Finally, of course, framing is a vital element in visionary leadership. Shared visions are achieved through common framing.

There are five language forms that can help you frame issues— metaphors, jargon, contrast, spin, and stories.

Metaphors help us understand one thing in terms of another. They work well when the standard of comparison is well understood and links logically to something else. When a manufacturing executive describes his goal of having "our production process running like a fine Swiss watch," he is using a metaphor to help his employees envision his ideal.

Organizational leaders are fond of using *jargon*. This is language that is peculiar to a particular profession, organization, or specific program. It conveys accurate meaning only to those who know the vernacular. Microsoft employees know, for instance, that a "Blue Badge" is a permanent employee, while an "Orange Badge" designates a temp or independent contractor.

When leaders use the *contrast* technique, they illuminate a subject in terms of its opposite. Why? Because sometimes it's easier to say what a subject is *not* more easily than what it is. When an executive at a small pharmaceutical company was frustrated by his employees' lack of concern with keeping costs down, he constantly chided them with the phrase, "we're not Pfizer." The message he wanted to convey was that his company didn't have the financial resources of the drug giant and they needed to reduce costs.

Presidential politics has created a new term: *spin*. The objective of this technique is to cast your subject in a positive or negative light. Leaders who are good at "spinning" get others to interpret their interests in positive terms and opposing interests in negative terms. During the 2012 U.S. presidential campaign, Democratic leaders regularly used spin to describe Republican Mitt Romney as an insensitive multimillionaire "who is out of touch with the middle class."

Finally, leaders use *stories* to frame issues with examples that are larger than metaphors or jargon. When leaders at 3M tell the story of how Post-it Notes were discovered, they remind people of the importance the company places on creativity and serendipity in the innovation process.

TRUTH

26

You Get What You
Expect

Let me tell you about 105 Israeli soldiers who were participating in a combat command course. The four instructors in this course were told that one-third of the specific incoming trainees had high potential, one-third had normal potential, and the potential of the rest was unknown. In reality, the trainees were randomly assigned into these categories by researchers conducting the study. In spite of the fact that the three groups should have performed about equally, since they were randomly placed, those trainees who instructors were told had high potential scored significantly higher on objective achievement tests, exhibited more positive attitudes, and held their leaders in higher regard than did the others.

What happened here illustrates the power of expectations. The instructors of the supposedly high-potential trainees got better results from them because the instructors expected it! This same result has been well documented in studies of teachers' behavior in classrooms. What teachers expect from students is what they generally get.

Think of expectations as sort of a self-fulfilling prophesy. Expectations of how someone is likely to act cause that person to fulfill the expectation. In business, this tells us that managers get the performance they expect. Treat people as losers, and they won't disappoint you. Treat them as capable individuals who can perform at the highest level, and they'll do their best to prove you right. Leaders who expect more get more!

> Treat people as losers, and they won't disappoint you.

Why do high employee expectations lead to higher performance? Because a leader's expectations influence the leader's behavior toward employees. Leaders allocate resources to employees in proportion to their expectations. They invest their best leadership in those they expect to perform best. Employees who a leader expects to do well receive more emotional support through nonverbal cues (like smiling and eye contact), more frequent and valuable feedback, more challenging goals, better training, and more desirable assignments. And leaders exhibit greater trust in these employees. These behaviors, in turn, lead to employees who are better trained, with better skills and job knowledge. In addition, a leader's support helps build employee confidence, which increases the employee's belief that he or she can succeed on the job.

Leaders who expect more get more!

The message here for leaders is that you should expect high performance from your employees. Tell them verbally and show them by your behavior that you believe in them. Let them know that you think they have untapped potential and that they can achieve more than they have. But don't expect *too much*. Sky-high expectations can be intimidating and demoralizing—leading to frustration, failure, and low expectations in the future. If you help employees achieve "small wins," they'll build their confidence and gradually raise their expectations over time.

27

Charisma Can Be Learned

There is an increasing amount of evidence that supports the value of charisma in leadership. Many of our most visible leaders, both past and present, have stood out for their charismatic qualities. They include individuals such as John F. Kennedy, Martin Luther King, Jr., Winston Churchill, Margaret Thatcher, Vince Lombardi, Steve Jobs, Richard Branson, Bill Clinton, and Mother Theresa.

What differentiates these charismatic leaders from their noncharismatic counterparts? Common characteristics of charismatic leaders include self-confidence, a strong vision that proposes a future better than the status quo, the ability to articulate the vision, strong convictions in the vision, and the willingness to enact radical change.

We used to think that charismatic leaders were born. However, recent evidence suggests otherwise. Individuals can be trained to exhibit charismatic behaviors and can thus enjoy the benefits that accompany being labeled "a charismatic leader." Here are some specific charismatic behaviors you can engage in:

> Individuals can be trained to exhibit charismatic behaviors and can thus enjoy the benefits that accompany being labeled "a charismatic leader."

- **Project a powerful, confident, and dynamic presence.** Use a captivating and engaging voice tone. Convey confidence. Talk directly to people, maintain direct eye contact, and hold your body posture in a way that says you're sure of yourself. Speak clearly, avoid stammering, and avoid sprinkling your sentences with noncontent phrases such as "uhhh" and "you know."

- **Articulate an overarching vision.** Create a vision for the future expressed as an idealized goal, specify unconventional ways of achieving the vision, and communicate the vision to others. The road to achieving the vision should be novel but appropriate to the context. And remember that success is not only having a vision but also being able to get others to buy into it.

■ **Communicate high performance expectations and confidence in others' ability to meet these expectations.** State ambitious goals for individuals and groups and demonstrate your belief that they will be achieved.

It's been shown that a person can learn to become charismatic by following a three-step process. First, you need to develop the aura of charisma by maintaining an optimistic view, using passion as a catalyst for generating enthusiasm, and communicating with the whole body, not just with words. Second, you have to draw others in by creating a bond that inspires others to follow. And third, you need to bring out the potential in followers by tapping into their emotions.

The preceding approach seems to work, as evidenced by the success researchers have had in actually scripting college students to "play" charismatic. The students were taught to articulate an overarching goal, to communicate high performance expectations, to exhibit confidence in the ability of subordinates to meet those expectations, and to empathize with the needs of their subordinates. They learned to project a powerful, confident, and dynamic presence, and they practiced using a captivating and engaging voice tone. To further capture the dynamics and energy of charisma, the leaders were trained to evoke charismatic nonverbal characteristics: They alternated between pacing and sitting on the edges of their desks, leaned toward the subordinates, maintained direct eye contact, and had a relaxed posture and animated facial expressions. These researchers found that these students could learn how to project charisma. Moreover, subordinates of these leaders had higher task performance, task adjustment, and adjustment to the leader and to the group than did subordinates who worked under groups led by noncharismatic leaders.

Researchers have been successful in actually scripting college students to "play" charismatic.

What this tells us is that while some people clearly have an intuitive style that creates charisma, you can train yourself to exhibit charismatic behaviors. And to the degree to which you're successful, you will be perceived by others as a charismatic leader.

28

Charisma Is Not Always an Asset

> **While the media tends to love charismatic leaders, charisma is not always needed nor an asset.**

If you have any doubts that there are negatives associated with charisma, let me just name three charismatic leaders: Adolph Hitler, Charles Manson, and Osama bin Laden. In addition, less well-known destructive charismatics include the "Queen of Mean" Leona Helmsley, Ken Lay and Jeff Skilling at the now defunct Enron, and Tyco's former CEO Dennis Kozlowski (who is serving an 8-to-25-year sentence in a New York prison).

Research tells us that charismatic leadership is not always needed to achieve high levels of employee performance. There are situations that favor it. Charisma appears to be most appropriate when the follower's task has an ideological component or when the environment involves a high degree of stress and uncertainty. This may explain why, when charismatic leaders surface, it's more likely to be in politics, religion, war time, or when a business firm is in its infancy or facing a life-threatening crisis. In the 1930s, Franklin D. Roosevelt offered a vision to get Americans out of the Great Depression. In 1997, when Apple was floundering and lacking direction, the board persuaded cofounder Steve Jobs to return as interim CEO to inspire the company to return to its innovative roots.

In addition to ideology and environmental uncertainty, another situational factor limiting charisma appears to be level in the organization. As noted in Truth 27, "Charisma Can Be Learned," the creation of a vision is a key component of charisma. But visions typically apply to entire organizations or major divisions. They tend to be created by top executives. As such, charisma probably has more direct relevance to explaining the success and failures of chief executives than of first-line supervisors.

And then there is the dark side of charisma. Those charismatic leaders, who are larger than life, often don't act in the best interests of their organizations. Many use their power to remake their organizations in their own image. They often blur the boundary separating their personal interests from their organization's interests. And at its worst, the perils of this ego-driven charisma are leaders who allow their self-interest and

There is a dark side to charisma.

personal goals to override the goals of the organization. Intolerant of criticism, they surround themselves with yes-people who are rewarded for pleasing the leader and they create a climate in which people are afraid to question or challenge the "king" or "queen" when they think he or she is making a mistake.

The dark side of charisma reveals leaders who use power for personal gain, promote their own personal vision, stifle critical or opposing viewpoints, consider their decision insights superior to others, and who become insensitive to others' needs. They become egotistical, narcissistic, manipulative, and often ruthless. The same confidence, drive, communication skills, and charm that led to a positive charismatic persona become a powerful aphrodisiac driven by self-interest.

A study of 29 companies that went from good to great (their cumulative stock returns were all at least three times better than the general stock market over 15 years) found an *absence* of ego-driven charismatic leaders. Although the leaders of these firms were fiercely ambitious and driven, their ambition was directed toward their company rather than themselves. They generated extraordinary results, but with little fanfare or hoopla. They took responsibility for mistakes and poor results but gave credit for successes to other people. They channeled their ego needs away from themselves and into the goal of building a great organization. This study is important because it confirms that leaders don't necessarily need to be charismatic to be effective, especially where charisma is enmeshed with an outsized ego.

> Leaders don't necessarily need to be charismatic to be effective.

29

Make Others
Dependent on You

Power is the capacity for a leader to influence the behavior of another individual or group of individuals so that they'll do something they wouldn't otherwise do. And as we'll show, effective leaders build a power base by making others dependent on them.

How do you make others dependent on you? There are two primary sources of power: your position in the organization and your personal characteristics.

In formal organizations, managerial positions come with authority—the right to give orders and expect the orders to be obeyed. In addition, a managerial position typically comes with the discretion to allocate rewards and enact punishments. Managers can give out desirable work assignments, appoint people to interesting or important projects, provide favorable performance reviews, and recommend salary increases. But they also can dish out undesirable work shifts and assignments, put people onto boring or low-profile projects, write up unfavorable appraisals, recommend undesirable transfers or even demotions, and limit merit raises.

You don't have to be a manager or have formal authority to have power. You can influence others through personal characteristics such as your expertise or personal charisma. In today's high-tech world, expertise has become an increasingly powerful source of influence. As jobs have become more specialized and complex, organizations have become dependent on experts with special skills or knowledge to achieve goals. Specialists such as software programmers, tax accountants, environmental engineers, and industrial psychologists are examples of individuals in organizations who can wield power as a result of their expertise. If you're director of human resources in your firm and you need valid selection tests to help you identify high-potential candidates—and you rely on the industrial psychologist on your staff to provide these valid tests—that industrial psychologist has expert power. Of course, charisma is also a powerful source of influence. If you possess charismatic traits, you can use this power to get others to do what you want.

> You don't have to be a manager or have formal authority to have power.

The key to gaining power is making others dependent on you. And how do you do that? By gaining control over resources that are important and scarce.

If nobody wants what you've got, it's not going to create dependency. To create dependency, therefore, the thing(s) you control must be perceived as being important. It's been found, for instance, that organizations actively seek to avoid uncertainty. We should, therefore, expect that those individuals or groups who can reduce an organization's uncertainty will be perceived as controlling an important resource. For instance, during a labor strike, the organization's negotiating representatives have increased power. And engineers, as a group, are more powerful at Intel than at Procter & Gamble. An organization such as Intel, which is heavily technologically oriented, is highly dependent on its engineers to maintain its products' technical advantages and quality. And, at Intel, engineers are clearly a powerful group. At Procter & Gamble, marketing is the name of the game, and marketers are the most powerful occupational group. These examples support not only the view that the ability to reduce uncertainty increases a group's importance, and hence its power, but also the view that what's important is situational. It varies among organizations and undoubtedly also varies over time within any given organization.

If something is plentiful, possession of it will not increase your power. A resource needs to be perceived as scarce to create dependency. This can help to explain how low-ranking members in an organization, who have important knowledge not available to high-ranking members, gain power over the high-ranking members. It also helps to make sense out of behaviors of low-ranking members that otherwise might seem illogical, such as destroying the procedure manuals that describe how a job is done, refusing to train people in their jobs or even to show others exactly what they do, creating specialized language and terminology that inhibit others from understanding their jobs, or operating in secrecy so an activity will appear more complex and difficult than it really is.

> If something is plentiful, possession of it will not increase your power.

TRUTH

30

Successful Leaders Are Politically Adept

When people in organizations convert their power into action, we describe them as engaged in politics. Those with good political skills have the ability to use their power bases effectively. And effective leaders know how to be politically adept.

Politics refers to those activities that are not required as part of an individual's formal role but that influence, or attempt to influence, the distribution of advantages and disadvantages within the organization. Politicking is outside your specified job requirements. And it includes a wide range of behaviors—including building relationships with people inside and outside the organization who can provide useful information or assistance, avoiding fights over issues that aren't critical, withholding key information from decision makers, joining a coalition, spreading rumors, exchanging favors with others in the organization for mutual benefit, lobbying on behalf or against a particular individual or decision alternative, and promoting your contributions and accomplishments.

To many, playing organizational politics is seen negatively. They may even be proud of the fact that they don't "play politics." They think they can succeed in the organization on their job performance alone. But they're naïve. Politics are part of organizational life.

Politics are part of organizational life.

For leaders, it's often necessary to play politics to get those things you want for your work team, department, or group. In fact, many leaders have failed, or seriously suboptimized their performance, because they either chose not to play politics or played it poorly.

There is a substantial amount of evidence demonstrating that political skill is a valid predictor of performance ratings. And it predicts both job performance and performance ratings in jobs that emphasize interpersonal and social requirements. So while good political skills might minimally enhance the performance of software programmers, they become incredibly important for the performance of sales jobs and project team leaders.

An excellent example of politics is the use of language by organization members. As we noted in Truth 25, "Effective Leaders Know How to Frame Issues," words frame issues. So, for instance, one person's *demonstration of loyalty* is another's *apple polishing*. When an executive pushes a decision downward in the organization, is she *delegating authority* or *passing the buck*? *Carefully documenting decisions* might be seen by others as *covering your rear*. These examples illustrate how the language of politics can be used to frame the most basic parts of a manager's job.

Are there any personality types that are better than others at developing their political skills? The answer is "yes." Your political "talent" is likely to be enhanced if you rate high on emotional intelligence (EI) and self-monitoring. EI refers to the ability to read and understand one's own and others' emotions. So individuals with high EI are able to assess what emotions are appropriate in a given situation and then control those emotions. They are also able to interpret others' emotions so as to exhibit the appropriate response. Bill Clinton, who undoubtedly has a high EI, demonstrated his skill in his famous "I feel your pain" statement.

People who are high self-monitors are able to adjust their behavior to changing situations, while low self-monitors tend to display their true feelings in every situation. High self-monitors are very sensitive to external cues and can behave differently in different situations, sometimes presenting striking contradictions between their public persona and their private self. Not surprising, this ability to conform to changing situations allows them to be social chameleons, adapting their behavior and attitudes to fit the people around them. One interesting study dramatically demonstrated the value of being a high self-monitor. It found that high self-monitors took an average of just 18 months to infiltrate the nucleus of their workplace network. In contrast, it took low self-monitors a staggering 13 years!

There is a substantial amount of evidence demonstrating that political skill is a valid predictor of performance ratings.

TRUTH

31

Ethical Leadership

Unethical practices by executives at organizations as varied as Enron, HealthSouth, Countrywide Financial, Berkshire Hathaway, Fannie Mae, AIG, and News Corp. have increased the need to consider ethical standards when evaluating a leader's effectiveness.

Ethics touches on leadership at a number of junctures. For instance, charisma has an ethical component. Unethical leaders are more likely to use their charisma to enhance *power over* followers, directed toward self-serving ends. Ethical leaders use their charisma in a socially constructive way to serve others. Leaders who treat their followers with fairness, especially by providing honest, frequent, and accurate information, are seen as more effective. Leaders rated highly ethically tend to have followers who are willing to put in the extra effort to ensure work is done properly and on time; and who then experience psychological well-being and high job satisfaction. There is also the issue of abuse of power by leaders when they give themselves large salaries, bonuses, and stock options while, at the same time, they seek to cut costs by laying off long-time employees. And the topic of trust explicitly deals with honesty and integrity in leadership. Because top executives set the moral tone for an organization, they need to set high ethical standards, demonstrate those standards through their own behavior, and encourage and reward integrity in others.

Leadership effectiveness needs to address the *means* that a leader uses in trying to achieve goals as well as the *content* of those goals. For instance, the late Steve Jobs was regularly characterized accurately as both a genius and charismatic leader. He was also rude, fiercely demanding, uncompromising, a bully, and the poster-boy for control freaks. He led Apple to the pinnacle of

Ethics touches on leadership at a number of junctures.

success; in the spring of 2012 it was the most valuable company in America. But the company's success was achieved by means of a ruthless work culture. Apple has frequently been described as a brutal and unforgiving place, where perfection is expected and accountability strictly enforced. Importantly, Apple's culture mirrors the personality of Jobs: ruthless, intense, unforgiving, and obsessed with perfection.

In addition, ethical leadership must address the content of a leader's goals. Are the changes that the leader seeks for the organization morally acceptable? Is a business leader effective if he or she builds an organization's success by selling products that damage the health of its users? This question, for example, might be asked of executives in the tobacco and junk food industries. Or is a military leader successful by winning a war that should not have been fought in the first place?

Leadership is not value-free.

Leadership is not value-free. As a leader, you should be prepared to be judged by both the means you use to achieve your goals and the moral content of those goals.

32

Virtual Leadership: Leading from Afar

How do you lead people who are physically separated from you and with whom you communicate electronically?

We can't ignore the reality that today's managers and their employees are increasingly being linked by networks rather than geographical proximity. Emerging technologies are allowing people to work from almost any location. Obvious examples include managers who regularly use e-mail to communicate with their staff, managers overseeing virtual projects or teams, and managers whose telecommuting employees are linked to the office by a computer at home. These managers need to become effective virtual leaders—who use e-mail, tweets, phone conferences, Web-enabled meetings, and technologies such as Skype and FaceTime to communicate effectively.

What's missing in virtual interactions that provide challenges to the virtual leader? There's a lack of physical contact, it's difficult to achieve work group cohesion, there is no opportunity for direct supervision, and there is often a time difference. But the central issue is communication.

> Today's managers and their employees are increasingly being linked by networks.

In face-to-face communications, harsh words can be softened by nonverbal action. A smile and supporting body language, for instance, can lessen the blow behind strong words like *disappointed*, *unsatisfactory*, *inadequate*, or *below expectations*. That nonverbal component doesn't exist online or in a phone call. Because such communications lack emotions and feelings, an e-mail or tweet exchange can easily lead to escalations of conflicts that would never occur had the parties been face-to-face. Online leaders also need to be sure the tone of their message correctly reflects the emotions they want to send. Is the message formal or informal? Does it match the verbal style of the sender? Does it convey the appropriate level of importance or urgency? And online leaders need to choose an appropriate style of communication. Many inexperienced virtual leaders use the same style with their bosses that they're using with their staff, with unfortunate consequences. Or they're selectively using digital communications to "hide" when delivering bad news.

Any discussion of virtual leadership needs to also consider the possibility that the digital age can turn nonleaders into leaders. Some managers whose face-to-face leadership skills are less than satisfactory may shine online. Their talents may lie in their writing skills and ability to read the messages behind written communiqués. A virtual environment works *against* people with strong verbal skills and *for* those with writing skills.

Finally, there is the challenge of developing effective virtual interpersonal skills. The idea of virtual interpersonal skills may, at first glance, seem like an oxymoron. *Interpersonal skills* implies social interaction. *Virtual* refers to a decoupling of space where events happen. But virtual leaders do need interpersonal skills—except they're just different from those required for face-to-face contacts. Virtual interpersonal skills are likely to include the abilities to communicate support and leadership through written words on a computer, smart phone, or iPad; to read emotions in others' written messages; and to develop good phone skills. For the virtual leader, good writing skills are rapidly becoming an extension of interpersonal skills.

> A virtual environment works *against* people with strong verbal skills and *for* those with writing skills.

33

Adjust Your Leadership Style for Cultural Differences, or When in Rome…

Many managers fail as leaders because they forget to adjust their style for the cultural background of their employees. This applies to managers who take on assignments in a foreign country as well as managers who find themselves overseeing employees who come from a different cultural background. Research has found that national culture directly shapes a manager's effectiveness and what matters most is the manager's choice of leadership preferences and communication styles.

National culture affects leadership style in two ways. It shapes the preferences of leaders, and it also defines what's acceptable to subordinates. Leaders can't choose their styles at will. They're constrained by the cultural conditions in which they have been socialized and that their subordinates have come to expect. For example, a manipulative or autocratic style is compatible with societies in which there is a great deal of power inequality, and we find this in Arab and Latin American countries. Arab leaders are expected to be tough and strong. To show kindness or to be generous without being asked to do so is perceived as a sign of weakness. In Mexico, with its strong paternalistic tradition and the presence of machismo values, leaders are expected to be decisive and autocratic. Power inequality ratings should also be a good indicator of employee willingness to accept participative leadership. Participation is likely to be most effective in countries that value equality, such as Norway, Finland, Denmark, and Sweden.

> National culture directly shapes a manager's effectiveness.

Leaders also need to take into consideration the expectations of their employees, even in their own countries, if those employees were raised in another culture. So a manager working in Los Angeles who is overseeing a group of employees who were born and raised in Mexico might be most effective if he biases his style toward being more autocratic. This is the style his employees are more used to in their homeland, may be closer to their expectations, and is most likely to be associated by employees with effective leadership.

A final note on cultural differences. Remember that most leadership theories were developed in the United States, by Americans, with American subjects. That means they will have a U.S. bias. They emphasize follower responsibilities rather than rights; assume hedonism rather than commitment to duty or altruistic motivation; assume centrality of work and democratic value orientation; and stress rationality rather than spirituality, religion, or superstition. These assumptions don't apply universally. For instance, this doesn't describe India, which places a great deal more emphasis on spirituality. It doesn't describe Japan, where great concern is given toward ensuring that employees are able to "save face." And it doesn't apply in China, where it's acceptable to publicly humiliate employees. Executives at the highly successful Asia Department Store in central China are a case in point. They blatantly brag about practicing "heartless" management, require new employees to undergo two to four weeks of military training with units of the People's Liberation Army to increase their obedience, and conduct the store's in-house training sessions in a public place where employees can openly suffer embarrassment from their mistakes. This approach clearly would not be well received in countries like Canada, Great Britain, or Japan.

> Most leadership theories were developed in the United States.... They have a U.S. bias.

TRUTH

34

Hearing
Isn't Listening

Many managers hear very well but don't listen. Confused? Let me explain. Hearing is merely picking up sound vibrations. Listening is making sense out of what we hear. That is, listening requires paying attention, interpreting, and remembering sound stimuli.

Effective listening is active rather than passive. In passive listening, you're like a recorder. You absorb the information given. Active listening, in contrast, requires you to "get inside" the speaker's head so that you can understand the communication from his or her point of view. As an active listener, you try to understand what the speaker wants to communicate rather than what you want to understand. You also demonstrate acceptance of what is being said. You listen objectively without judging content. Finally, as an active listener, you take responsibility for completeness. You do whatever is necessary to get the fully intended meaning from the speaker's communication.

> Hearing is merely picking up sound vibrations. Listening is making sense out of what we hear.

The following eight behaviors are associated with effective active-listening skills. If you want to improve your listening skills—and every manager should—look to these behaviors as guides:

> Effective listening is active rather than passive.

1. **Make eye contact.** How do you feel when somebody doesn't look at you when you're speaking? If you're like most people, you're likely to interpret this behavior as aloofness or lack of interest.

2. **Exhibit affirmative head nods and appropriate facial expressions.** The effective listener shows interest in what is being said. How? Through nonverbal signals. Affirmative head nods and appropriate facial expressions, when added to good eye contact, convey to the speaker that you're listening.

3. **Avoid distracting actions or gestures.** The other side of showing interest is avoiding actions that suggest that your mind is somewhere else. When listening, don't look at your watch, shuffle papers, or engage in similar distractions. They make the speaker feel as if you're bored or uninterested and indicate that you aren't fully attentive.

4. **Ask questions.** The critical listener analyzes what he or she hears and asks questions. This behavior provides clarification, ensures understanding, and assures the speaker that you're listening.

5. **Paraphrase.** Restate what the speaker has said in your own words. The active listener uses phrases such as "What I hear you saying is…" or "Do you mean…?" By rephrasing what the speaker has said in your own words and feeding it back to the speaker, you verify the accuracy of your understanding.

6. **Avoid interrupting the speaker.** Let the speaker complete his or her thought before you try to respond. Don't try to second-guess where the speaker's thoughts are going. When the speaker is finished, you'll know it!

7. **Don't overtalk.** Although talking may be more fun and silence may be uncomfortable, you can't talk and listen at the same time. The active listener recognizes this fact and doesn't overtalk.

8. **Make smooth transitions between the roles of speaker and listener.** In most situations, you're continually shifting back and forth between the roles of speaker and listener. The active listener makes transitions smoothly from speaker to listener and back to speaker. From a listening perspective, this means concentrating on what a speaker has to say and avoiding thoughts about what you're going to say as soon as you get your chance.

TRUTH

35

Listen to the
Grapevine

Some years back, the rumor mill was especially active at Coca-Cola's Atlanta headquarters. The company was in the midst of a major reorganization that had included 5,200 layoffs worldwide earlier in the year. Rumors were saying that key executives were leaving, that there were ongoing turf wars among senior executives, and that more layoffs were pending. These rumors were beginning to seriously undermine morale at Coke. In an attempt to shut down the rumor mill, the company's executive vice president tried to set things straight. He acknowledged that the company's senior management hadn't done a good enough job of telling employees about the changes that were taking place. He pledged "better and more frequent communication."

As executives at Coke have learned, rumors can be a major distraction for employees. This doesn't mean that management can ever eliminate the grapevine. But certain conditions tend to stimulate grapevine activity. And importantly, as executives at Coke did, management needs to monitor the grapevine and respond to the issues with which it's concerned.

Rumors in the workplace perform a number of purposes. They structure and reduce anxiety. They make sense of limited or fragmented information. They serve as a vehicle to organize group members into coalitions. And they signal a sender's status ("I'm an insider and you're not!") or power ("I have the power to make you an insider.").

Studies have found that rumors emerge as a response to situations that are important to us, where there is ambiguity, and under conditions that arouse anxiety. Work situations frequently contain these three elements, which explains why rumors flourish in organizations. The secrecy and competition that typically prevail in large organizations—around issues such as appointment of new bosses, relocation of offices, realignment of

Rumors emerge as a response to situations that are important to us, where there is ambiguity, and under conditions that arouse anxiety.

work assignments, and layoffs—create conditions that encourage and sustain rumors on the grapevine.

Accept the fact that the grapevine isn't going to go away. It's an important part of any group's or organization's communication system. Astute managers acknowledge the existence of the grapevine and use it in beneficial ways. They use it to identify issues that employees consider important and that are likely to create anxiety. They view it as both a filter and feedback mechanism by highlighting issues that employees consider relevant. For instance, the grapevine can tap employee concerns. If the grapevine is carrying a rumor of a mass layoff, and if you know the rumor is totally false, the message still has meaning. It reflects the fears and concerns of employees and, hence, should not be ignored. Importantly, managers can actually manage the grapevine by planting messages that it wants employees to hear. Managers should monitor grapevine patterns and observe which individuals are interested in what issues and who is likely to actively pass along rumors. In addition, managers need to reduce the negative consequences that rumors can create. If you come across an active rumor and think it has the potential to be destructive, consider how you might lessen its impact by improving organizational communication. This could include announcing timetables for making important decisions; explaining decisions and behaviors that may appear inconsistent or secretive; emphasizing the downside, as well as the upside, of current decisions and future plans; and openly discussing worst-case possibilities.

> Astute managers acknowledge the existence of the grapevine and use it in beneficial ways.

36

Men and Women Communicate Differently

Research confirms what many of us have thought true since our adolescent days: Men and women often have difficulty communicating with each other. The reason? They use conversation for different purposes. Men tend to use talk to emphasize status, while women generally use it to create connection. These differences create real challenges for managers.

Communication is a continual balancing act, juggling the conflicting needs for intimacy and independence. Intimacy emphasizes closeness and commonalties. Independence emphasizes separateness and differences. But men and women handle these conflicts differently. Women speak and hear a language of connection and intimacy, while men speak and hear a language of status, power, and independence. So, for many men, conversations are primarily a means to preserve independence and maintain status in a hierarchical social order. For many women, conversations are negotiations for closeness in which people try to seek and give confirmation and support. Here are some examples.

Men tend to use talk to emphasize status, while women generally use it to create connection.

Men frequently complain that women ramble on and on about their problems. Women criticize men for not listening. What's happening is that when men hear a problem, they frequently assert their desire for independence and control by offering solutions. Many women, on the other hand, view telling a problem as a means to promote closeness. The women present the problem to gain support and connection, not to get the man's advice. Mutual understanding is symmetrical; but giving advice is asymmetrical—it sets up the advice giver as more knowledgeable and more in control. This contributes to distancing men and women in their efforts to communicate.

Men are often more direct than women in conversation. A man might say, "I think you're wrong on that point." A woman might say, "Have you looked at the marketing department's research report on that point?" (the implication being that the report will show the error). Men frequently see female indirectness as "covert" or "sneaky," but women are not as concerned as men with the status and one-upmanship that directness often creates.

Women tend to be less boastful than men. They often downplay their authority or accomplishments to avoid appearing as braggarts and to take the other person's feelings into account. However, men can frequently misinterpret this and incorrectly conclude that a woman is less confident and competent than she really is.

Men often criticize women for seeming to apologize all the time. For instance, men tend to see the

Women tend to be less boastful than men.

phrase "I'm sorry" as a weakness because they interpret the phrase to mean the woman is accepting blame, when he knows she's not to blame. The woman also knows she's not to blame. The problem is that women frequently use "I'm sorry" to express regret and restore balance to a conversation: "I know you must feel badly about this; I do, too." For many women, "I'm sorry" is an expression of understanding and caring about the other person's feelings rather than an apology.

37

What You Do Overpowers What You Say

It's not what you say, it's what you do! Actions DO speak louder than words.

When faced with inconsistencies between words and actions, people tend to give greater credence to actions. It's behavior that counts!

The implication of this for managers is: You're a role model. Employees will imitate your behavior and attitudes. They watch what their boss does and then imitate or adapt accordingly. This doesn't mean, however, that words fall on deaf ears. Words can influence others. But when words and actions diverge, people focus most on what they see in terms of behavior.

Actions DO speak louder than words.

To illustrate, consider your attitude toward employees and your ethical behavior. Many managers will pontificate on the importance of their employees: "It's people that make the difference here" or "People are our most important asset." Then they engage in practices that contradict this attitude. For instance, they don't listen to employees' complaints, they're insensitive to employee personal problems, or they let good people leave for other jobs without making a concerted effort to keep them. When employees see contradictions between words and actions, they're most likely to believe the *actions* of managers regardless of what they hear those managers say. Similarly, managers who want to establish a strong ethical climate in their workplaces need to make sure their deeds match their words. Talk about high standards of integrity will fall on deaf ears if they're uttered by managers who pad their expense account, take office supplies home for personal use, or regularly come in late to work or leave early. Enron, for instance, had a 64-page in-house "Code of Ethics" booklet that was supposed to provide a moral guide for how employees should conduct the energy firm's business affairs. But employees took their cues from the behavior of Enron's top executives. These executives consistently engaged in self-serving financial dealings, conflicts of interest, and exploitation of customers. Employees saw these practices and basically ignored the firm's Code of Ethics.

Contradictions between words and actions can be most damaging to a manager's attempt to build trust with his or her employees. A manager who is trusted is one who can be depended on not to take advantage of people or situations. It's hard for employees to trust a manager who says one thing but does another.

There is an obvious exception to the previous findings. An increasing number of leaders have developed

Contradictions between words and actions can be most damaging to a manager's attempt to build trust with his or her employees.

the skill of shaping words and putting the proper "spin" on situations so that others focus on the leaders' words rather than the behavior. Successful politicians seem particularly adept at this skill. Why people believe these spins when faced with conflicting behavioral evidence is not clear. But it certainly underscores the power of words to shape people's opinions. Do we want to believe that our leaders would not lie to us? Do we want to believe what politicians say, especially when we hold them in high regard? Do we give high-status people, for whom we've previously given our vote, the benefit of the doubt when confronted with their negative behavior? These are questions that, at least at this time, we don't have answers to.

TRUTH

38

The Value of Silence

Sherlock Holmes once solved a murder mystery based not on what happened but on what didn't happen. Holmes remarked to his assistant, Dr. Watson, about "the curious incident of the dog in the nighttime." Watson, surprised, responded, "But the dog did nothing in the nighttime." To which Holmes replied, "That was the curious incident." Holmes concluded the crime had to be committed by someone with whom the dog was familiar because the watchdog didn't bark.

The dog that didn't bark in the night is often used as a metaphor for an event that is significant by reason of its absence. That story is also an excellent illustration of the importance of silence in communication.

Silence—defined here as an absence of speech or noise—has been generally ignored as a form of communication because it represents an *in*action or nonevent. But it's not necessarily inaction. Nor is silence, as many believe, a failure to communicate. It can, in fact, be a powerful form of communication. It can mean someone is thinking or contemplating a response to a question. It can mean a person is anxious and fearful of speaking. It can signal agreement, dissent, frustration, or anger.

Silence can be a powerful form of communication.

We can see several links between silence and behavior at work. For instance, silence is a critical element in groupthink, in which it implies agreement with the majority. It can be a way for employees to express dissatisfaction, as when they "suffer in silence." It can be a sign that someone is upset, as when a typically talkative person suddenly says nothing—"What's the matter with him? Is he all right?" It's a powerful tool used by managers to signal disfavor by shunning or ignoring employees with "silent insults." And it's a crucial element of group decision making, allowing individuals to think over and contemplate what others have said.

Sometimes the
real message in a
communication
is buried in the
silence.

Failing to pay close attention to the silent portion of a conversation can result in missing a vital part of the message. Astute communicators watch for gaps, pauses, and hesitations. They hear and interpret silence. They treat pauses, for instance, as analogous to a flashing yellow light at an intersection—they pay attention to what comes next. Is the person thinking, deciding how to frame an answer? Is the person fearful of speaking up? Sometimes the real message in a communication is buried in the silence.

39

Watch Out for Digital Distractions

Today's workplace is full of digital distractions. As one executive recently put it, "No one has time to do any work. They're all too busy texting, instant messaging, e-mailing, or on their iPad's updating their Facebook page, watching YouTube videos, shopping online, playing Angry Birds, or engaged in some other crazy time-waster."

To quote an old comic strip, "we have met the enemy and he is us." We've become addicted to technology but not necessarily in ways that enhance work performance. What was originally created to either improve work communication or meant to be used outside the workplace has now turned into a management nightmare. As one manager put it, "How do you get people to get any work done when they have to check their iPhones every 10 minutes?"

> We've become addicted to technology but not necessarily in ways that enhance work performance.

Work interruptions have been defined as "incidents or occurrences that impede or delay organizational members as they attempt to make progress on their work tasks." This definition is broad and includes phone calls, text messages, unexpected meetings, and coworker conversations. But our concern is with digital work interruptions. Employees and managers, alike, have always had to contend with interruptions at work. Now, however, as computers, smart phones, iPads, and the Internet have become part of many jobs, and an essential element of most people's lives, digital interruptions have become an increasing threat to worker productivity.

Is there a positive benefit to digital interruptions at work? Surprisingly, several experts think so. Especially as related to knowledge workers, positive benefits might include providing mental breaks that allow employees to return to tasks more alert, restoring mental capacity, and fostering feelings of autonomy. However, most of the evidence suggests that the negatives trump the benefits. For instance, one study found 53 percent of employees waste at least one hour a day due to all types of distractions, and 45 percent work only 15 minutes or less without getting interrupted. Another put the cost of collaboration and social tools at $10,375 per year annually in wasted productivity, based on an average wage of $30 an hour. Still another study calculates that $650 billion is lost in the United States each year due to unnecessary interruptions. And that number is increasing by about 5 percent a year. While much of these costs are due to meetings, phone calls, and other nondigital interruptions, a good portion is directly due to technology. One recent study, in fact, attributed nearly 60 percent of work interruptions to digital distractions such as e-mail, personal online activities, IM, text messaging, and Web searching.

It can help to better understand digital interruptions by looking at research on addiction. Human beings seem to have a propensity to become addicted. One group of researchers asserts that as many as 47 percent of the U.S. adult population suffers from maladaptive signs of an addictive disorder over any 12-month period. That, of course, includes everything from tobacco to pornography. But what about Internet addiction? The evidence indicates that Internet addiction generally attacks about the same proportion of the population as gambling or alcohol addiction. About 10 percent of Internet users have some form of dependency on the technology.

> **About 10 percent of Internet users have some form of dependency on the technology.**

The preceding suggests that while only a minority of employees might suffer from Internet addiction, it's not irrelevant. And just as an open bottle of wine can be a powerful distraction to an alcoholic, easy Internet access or a Blackberry sitting on a desk can be an enticing distraction for many employees.

Is there anything management can do to discourage digital interruptions in the workplace? A few solutions have been offered, but all face the increasing realization that human beings are easily distracted and that technologies like the Internet, e-mail, and smart phones have strong addictive properties.

Given the preceding caveat, here are a few suggestions. Managers should consider instituting specific policies that clarify the extent that computers, smart phones, iPads, and the like can be used during work hours for personal activities. This is often part of a program that includes training so employees understand how digital interruptions can undermine work productivity. For instance, it has been found that the optimal number for checking e-mails is four times a day. Employees often don't realize that there is little to be gained by checking it more often. Other suggestions include tracking online usage patterns of employees or, in cases where abuse is extensive, blocking access to social networks and nonbusiness websites on the organization's computers.

TRUTH

40

What We Know That Makes Teams Work

Teams have become an essential device for structuring job activities. But how do managers create effective teams?

The key components making up effective teams can be subsumed into four general categories: *work design*, team *composition*, resources and other *contextual* influences, and *process* variables that reflect the things that go on in the team.

Teams have become an essential device for structuring job activities.

Work Design. Teams work best when employees have freedom and autonomy, the opportunity to utilize different skills and talents, the ability to complete a whole and identifiable task or product, and a task or project that has a substantial impact on others. The evidence indicates that these characteristics increase members' sense of responsibility and ownership over the work and make the work more interesting to perform.

Composition. To perform effectively, a team requires three different types of skills. It needs people with *technical expertise*. It needs people with *problem-solving and decision-making skills*. And teams need people with good listening, feedback, conflict resolution, and other *interpersonal skills*.

Personality has a significant influence on team behavior. Specifically, teams that rate higher in average levels of extraversion, agreeableness, conscientiousness, and emotional stability (see Truth 4, "When In Doubt Hire Conscientious People!") tend to receive higher managerial ratings for team performance.

The most effective teams are neither very small (under 4 or 5) or very large (over a dozen). Very small teams are likely to lack for diversity of views, and teams of more than 12 have difficulty getting much done.

Teams made up of flexible individuals have members who can complete each other's tasks. This is an obvious plus to a team because it greatly improves its adaptability and makes it less reliant on any single member.

Not every employee is a team player. When people who would prefer to work alone are required to team up, there is a direct threat to the team's morale. This suggests that, when team members are selected, individual preferences be considered as well as abilities, personalities, and skills.

Context. The three contextual factors that appear to be most significantly related to team performance are the presence of adequate resources, effective leadership, and a performance evaluation and reward system that reflects team contributions.

Work groups are part of a larger organization system. As such, all work teams rely on resources outside the group to sustain it. And a scarcity of resources directly reduces the ability of the team to perform its job effectively. Supportive resources include timely information, equipment, adequate staffing, encouragement, and administrative assistance.

Team members must agree on who is to do what and ensure that all members contribute equally in sharing the workload. In addition, the team needs to determine how schedules will be set, what skills need to be developed, how the group will resolve conflicts, and how the group will make and modify decisions. Agreeing on the specifics of work and how they fit together to integrate individual skills requires team leadership and structure.

How do you get team members to be both individually and jointly accountable? The traditional, individually oriented evaluation and reward system needs to be modified to reflect team performance. In addition to evaluating and rewarding employees for their individual contributions, management should consider group-based appraisals, small-group incentives, and other system modifications that will reinforce team effort and commitment.

> Agreeing on the specifics of work and how they fit together to integrate individual skills requires team leadership and structure.

Process. The final category related to team effectiveness is process variables. They include member commitment to a common purpose, establishment of specific team goals, effective information sharing, and a managed level of conflict.

Effective teams put a tremendous amount of effort into agreeing on a common and meaningful purpose that provides direction, momentum, and commitment for members.

Successful teams translate their common purpose into specific, measurable, and realistic performance goals. These goals help teams maintain their focus on getting results.

To achieve high-quality solutions, team members need to effectively integrate diverse information sets. Information sharing is the central process through which team members collectively use their available information resources.

Too much conflict can hinder team performance. But conflict on a team isn't necessarily bad. Conflict can improve team effectiveness when it stimulates discussion, promotes critical assessment of problems and options, and leads to better team decisions.

TRUTH

41

2 + 2 Doesn't Necessarily Equal 4

Proponents of teams frequently say that one of the reasons business firms should organize around teams is that they create positive synergy. That is, the cumulative productivity output of a team is greater than would occur if individual members had worked alone because the sense of team spirit spurs individual effort. So 2 + 2 can equal 5. The truth is that teams often create negative synergy. Some individuals expend less effort when working collectively than when working individually, so 2 + 2 can equal 3! The reason for this negative outcome? It's called *social loafing*.

In the late 1920s, a German psychologist named Max Ringelmann compared the results of individual and group performance on a rope-pulling task. He expected that the group's effort would be equal to the sum of the efforts of individuals within the group. For instance, three people pulling together should exert three times as much pull on the rope as one person, and eight people should exert eight times as much pull. Ringelmann's results, however, didn't confirm his expectations. Groups of three people exerted a force only two-and-a-half times the average individual performance. Groups of eight collectively achieved less than four times the solo rate.

> The truth is that teams often create *negative* synergy.

Replications of Ringelmann's research with similar tasks have generally supported his findings: Increases in group size are inversely related to individual performance. More may be better in the sense that the total productivity of a group of four is greater than that of one or two people, but the individual productivity of each group member declines.

What causes this social loafing effect? It may be due to a belief that others in the group are not carrying their fair share. If you see others as lazy or inept, you can re-establish equity by reducing your effort. Another explanation is dispersion of responsibility. Because the results of

Increases in group size are inversely related to individual performance.

the group cannot be attributed to any single person, the relationship between an individual's input and the group's output is clouded. In such situations, individuals may be tempted to become "free riders" and coast on the group's efforts. In other words, there will be a reduction in efficiency where individuals think that their contribution cannot be measured. Almost anyone who has been required to be part of a group project in school has typically seen the free-rider effect when all members of the project group share in a common grade. One or more group members will frequently contribute little and hide behind the hard work of others.

What are the implications of social loafing for the design of work teams? Where you use teams to enhance morale or improve coordination, you need to provide means for identifying and measuring individual efforts of members as well as the overall team's performance. If this isn't done, you have to weigh the potential losses in productivity from using groups against any possible gains in worker satisfaction.

TRUTH

42

The Value of Diversity on Teams

The past four decades have seen a marked increase in interest in workforce diversity. It's not unusual today for large organizations to have diversity goals, diversity initiatives, and diversity training. This focus on increasing workforce diversity can be largely traced back to the civil rights and women's liberation movements. The white, male-dominated organizations of the 1960s have given way to organizations that are diverse in terms of gender, race, and nationality. This begs the question: Are diverse teams as effective as their homogeneous counterparts?

Most team activities require a variety of skills and knowledge. Given this requirement, it would be reasonable to conclude that heterogeneous teams—those composed of dissimilar individuals—would be more likely to have diverse abilities and information and should be more effective. Research studies generally substantiate this conclusion, especially on cognitive, creativity-demanding tasks.

Most team activities require a variety of skills and knowledge.

When a team is diverse in terms of personality, gender, age, education, functional specialization, and experience, there is an increased probability that the team will possess the needed characteristics to complete its tasks effectively. The team may be more conflict-laden and less expedient as varied positions are introduced and assimilated, but the evidence generally supports the conclusion that heterogeneous teams perform more effectively than do those that are homogeneous. Essentially, diversity promotes conflict, which stimulates creativity, which leads to improved decision making.

But what about diversity created by racial or national differences? The evidence indicates that these elements of diversity interfere with team processes, at least in the short term. Cultural diversity seems to be an asset for tasks that call for a variety of viewpoints. But culturally heterogeneous teams have more difficulty in learning to work with each other and in solving problems. The good news is that these difficulties seem to dissipate with time. Although newly formed culturally diverse teams underperform newly formed culturally homogeneous teams, the differences disappear after about three months. The reason is that it takes culturally diverse teams a while to learn how to work through disagreements and different approaches to solving problems.

The evidence indicates that diversity interferes with team processes, at least in the short term.

So is diversity good for team and organization performance? In the longer term, the answer is probably "yes." At worst, permanent teams made up of diverse members don't underperform their homogeneous counterparts. In the short term, you need to differentiate efficiency and effectiveness. Diverse teams take longer to gel, so they're likely to be less efficient. But the results that diverse teams generate tend to be of a higher quality than those of homogeneous teams.

From a management perspective, you might consider purposely designing your work teams to include members who are "different" from the majority. They may be slower at doing their work, at least at the beginning, but you're likely to find the quality of their work and decisions to be high.

TRUTH

43

We're Not All Equal: Status Matters!

Many of us like to think that status isn't as important as it was a couple of generations ago. We can point to the hippie movement, equal rights legislation, the rapid growth of small entrepreneurial firms, flat organizations designed around teams, and technologies like e-mail and Twitter that bypass hierarchies as forces that have made organizations more egalitarian. The reality is that we continue to live in an essentially class-structured society.

Despite all attempts to make it more egalitarian, we have made little progress toward a classless society. Even the smallest group will develop roles, rights, and rituals to differentiate its members. And we're finding that even high-tech organizations that loathe formality and hierarchy adapt

> We continue to live in an essentially class-structured society.

mechanisms to create status differences. Take, for instance, e-mail. Here is a communication device that was touted as being able to democratize organizations. It allows people to communicate up and down hierarchical lines, unimpeded by gatekeepers and protocols. But you know what? Status differences have crept into the e-mail process. A study of some 30,000 e-mail messages at a high-tech firm that didn't use job titles, was organized around teams, and prided itself on democratic decision making provides interesting insights. People had found ways to create social distinctions. High-status employees tended to send short, curt messages, in part to minimize contact with lower-status workers but also to convey comfort with their own authority. In contrast, mid-status employees tended to produce long, argumentative messages loaded with jargon or overexplained answers to simple questions. And low-status employees' e-mails would contain non–work-related elements like forwarded jokes or happy-face emoticons. In addition, the study found that senior managers would take the longest to reply and had the poorest spelling and worst grammar—which all conveyed that they have better things to do with their time.

Status is an important factor in understanding human behavior because it's a significant motivator and can create major problems when people perceive status inequities. A fancy title, a large office, or even an impressive business card can carry a lot of weight in motivating employees.

Even the smallest group will develop roles and rituals to differentiate its members.

Conversely, a lack of status accoutrements can make people feel less important. Status inequities create frustration and can adversely influence employee performance and even lead to an unwanted resignation.

Keep in mind that the criteria that create status differ widely between cultures. For instance, status for Latin Americans and Asians tends to be derived from family position and formal roles held in organizations. In contrast, status in countries like the United States and Australia tends to be bestowed more on accomplishments than titles and family trees. The message here is to make sure you understand who and what holds status when interacting with people from a different culture than your own. An American manager who doesn't understand that office size is no measure of a Japanese executive's position or who fails to grasp the importance that the British place on family genealogy and social class is likely to unintentionally offend his Japanese or British counterpart and, in so doing, lessen his interpersonal effectiveness.

44

Not Everyone Is Team Material

Many people are not inherently team players. They are loners or people who want to be recognized for their individual achievements. There are also a great many organizations that have historically nurtured individual accomplishments. They have created competitive work environments where only the strong survive. If these organizations adopt teams, what can they do about the "I have to look out for me" employees that they created? And finally, countries differ in terms of their "groupiness." What if an organization wants to introduce teams into a work population that is made up largely of individuals born and raised in a highly individualistic society?

The previous points are meant to dramatize that one substantial barrier to using work teams is individual resistance. An employee's success is no longer defined in terms of individual performance. To perform well as team members, individuals must be able to communicate openly and honestly; to confront differences and resolve conflicts; and to sublimate personal goals for the good of the team. For many employees, these are difficult—sometimes impossible— tasks. As suggested in Truth 17, "Managing Across the Generation Gap," Baby Boomers might be more resistant to working in teams than younger workers because of having been raised in an environment that stressed individual achievement.

The challenge of creating team players will be greatest where (1) the national culture is highly individualistic and (2) the teams are being introduced into an established organization that has historically valued individual achievement. These conditions describe, for instance, what faced managers at AT&T, Ford, Motorola, and other large U.S.–based companies. These firms prospered by hiring and

> To perform well as team members, individuals must be able to communicate openly and honestly; to confront differences and resolve conflicts; and to sublimate personal goals for the good of the team.

rewarding corporate stars; they created a competitive climate that encouraged individual achievement and recognition. Employees in these types of firms can be jolted by a shift to the importance of team play. One veteran employee of a large company, who had done very well by working alone, described the experience of joining a team: "I'm learning my lesson. I just had my first negative performance appraisal in 20 years."

On the other hand, the challenge for management is less demanding when teams are introduced where employees have strong "group" values—such as in Japan or Mexico—or in new organizations that use teams as their initial form for structuring work. Mercedes-Benz's plant in Alabama, for instance, was designed around teams from its inception. Everyone at the plant was initially hired with the knowledge that they would be working in teams. And the ability to be a good team player was a basic hiring qualification that all new employees had to meet.

> The challenge for management is less demanding when teams are introduced where employees have strong "group" values.

The following summarizes the primary options managers have for trying to turn individuals into team players:

- **Selection**—Some people already possess the interpersonal skills to be effective team players. When hiring team members, in addition to the technical skills required to fill the job, care should be taken to ensure that candidates can fulfill their team roles as well as technical requirements.

- **Training**—A large proportion of people raised on the importance of individual accomplishment can be trained to become team players. Training specialists conduct exercises that allow employees to experience the satisfaction that teamwork can provide. They typically offer workshops to help employees improve their problem-solving, communication, negotiation, conflict-management, and coaching skills.

- **Rewards**—The reward system needs to be reworked to encourage cooperative efforts rather than competitive ones. Promotions, pay raises, and other forms of recognition should be given to individuals for how effective they are as collaborative team members.

   Unfortunately, in organizations that are undergoing the transformation to teams, there will likely be some current employees who will resist team training or prove untrainable. Your options with such individuals are essentially two. You can transfer them to another unit within the organization that does not have teams, if this possibility exists. The other choice is obvious and acknowledges that some employees may become casualties of the team approach.

TRUTH

45

The Case FOR Conflict

In our discussion of effective teams, we said that conflict isn't necessarily bad. Research tells us that there are three types of conflict: task, relationship, and process. Task conflict relates to the content and goals of the work. Relationship conflict focuses on interpersonal relationships. And process conflict relates to how work gets done. The evidence indicates that while relationship conflicts are almost always dysfunctional in groups or organizations, low levels of process and task conflict are often functional. Since many people seem to have difficulty with thinking of conflict in positive terms, let me make the argument to support the constructive side of conflict.

Conflict is constructive when it improves the quality of decisions, stimulates creativity and innovation, encourages interest and curiosity among group members, provides the medium through which problems can be aired and tensions released, and fosters an environment of self-evaluation and change. The evidence suggests that conflict can improve the quality of decision making by allowing all points, particularly the ones that are unusual or held by a minority, to be weighed in important decisions. Conflict is an antidote for groups that might be tempted to "rubber stamp" decisions that are based on weak assumptions, inadequate consideration of relevant alternatives, or other debilities. And conflict challenges the status quo and therefore furthers the creation of new ideas, promotes reassessment of group goals and activities, and increases the probability that a group will respond to change.

For an example of a company that has suffered because it has had too little functional conflict, you don't have to look further than General Motors. Many of GM's problems—from about 1970 up to its bankruptcy in 2009—can be traced to a lack of functional conflict. It hired and promoted individuals who were loyal "yes men." Managers were, for the most part, conservative white Anglo-Saxon males raised in the Midwestern United States and who resisted change. They were almost sanctimonious in their belief

Many of GM's problems—from about 1970 up to its bankruptcy in 2009—can be traced to a lack of functional conflict.

that what had worked in the past would continue to work in the future. Moreover, by sheltering executives in the company's Detroit offices and encouraging them to socialize with others inside the GM ranks, the company further insulated managers from conflicting perspectives.

There is substantial evidence indicating that conflict can be positively related to productivity. For instance, it was demonstrated that, among established groups, performance tended to improve more when there was conflict among members than when there was fairly close agreement. The investigators observed that when groups analyzed decisions that had been made by the individual members of that group, the average improvement among the high-conflict groups was 73 percent greater than that of those groups characterized by low-conflict conditions. Others have found similar results: Groups composed of members with different interests tend to produce higher-quality solutions to a variety of problems than do homogeneous groups.

As noted in Truth 42, "The Value of Diversity on Teams," evidence demonstrates that cultural diversity among group and organization members can increase creativity, improve the quality of decisions, and facilitate change by enhancing member flexibility. For example, researchers compared decision-making groups composed of all-Anglo individuals with groups that also contained members from Asian, Hispanic, and black ethnic groups. The ethnically diverse groups produced more effective and more feasible ideas and the unique ideas they generated tended to be of higher quality than the unique ideas produced by the all-Anglo group. Similarly, studies of systems analysts and research and development scientists support the

> Substantial evidence indicates that conflict can be positively related to productivity.

constructive value of conflict. An investigation of 22 teams of systems analysts found that the more incompatible groups were likely to be more productive. Research and development scientists have been found to be most productive where there is a certain amount of intellectual conflict.

TRUTH

46

Beware of Groupthink

If you're like me, you've occasionally felt like speaking up in a meeting or group setting but decided against it. Why didn't we speak up? If what we wanted to say didn't fit in with the dominant views of the group, we may have been victims of groupthink. This is a phenomenon that occurs when group members become so focused on achieving agreement that the search for consensus overrides any realistic assessment of deviant or unpopular views. It represents a deterioration in an individual's mental efficiency and reality testing as a result of group pressures.

We have all seen the symptoms of the groupthink phenomenon:

1. Group members rationalize any resistance to the assumptions that the group has made. No matter how strongly the evidence may contradict their basic assumptions, members behave so as to reinforce those assumptions continually.

2. Members apply direct pressure on those who momentarily express doubts about any of the group's shared views or who question the validity of arguments supporting the alternative favored by the majority.

3. Those members who have doubts or hold differing points of view seek to avoid deviating from what appears to be group consensus by keeping silent about misgivings and even minimizing to themselves the importance of their doubts.

4. There appears to be an illusion of unanimity. If someone doesn't speak, it's assumed that he or she sides with the majority view. In other words, abstention becomes viewed as a "Yes" vote.

In studies of historic American foreign policy decisions, groupthink symptoms were found to prevail when government policy-making groups failed: unpreparedness at Pearl Harbor in 1941, the U.S. invasion of North Korea, the Bay of Pigs fiasco, and the escalation of the Vietnam War. The *Challenger* space

In groupthink, if someone doesn't speak, it's assumed that he or she sides with the majority view.

shuttle disaster and the failure of the main mirror on the *Hubble* telescope have been linked to decision processes at NASA in which groupthink symptoms were evident. More recently, a U.S. Senate committee concluded that groupthink caused the CIA to interpret ambiguous data as conclusive evidence that Iraq had weapons of mass destruction.

Does groupthink attack all groups? No. It seems to occur most often where there is a clear group identity, where members hold a positive image of their group that they want to protect, and where

Groupthink is a means for a group to protect its positive image.

the group perceives a collective threat to this positive image. So groupthink is not a dissenter-suppression mechanism as much as it's a means for a group to protect its positive image. For instance, in the cases of the *Challenger* and *Hubble* fiascos, it was NASA's attempt to confirm its identity as "the elite organization that could do no wrong."

As a manager, what can you do to minimize groupthink? One thing you can do is play an impartial role when you're a group leader. You should actively seek input from all members and avoid expressing your own opinions, especially in the early stages of deliberation. Another thing is to appoint one group member to play the role of devil's advocate. This member's role is to openly challenge the majority position and offer divergent perspectives. Still another suggestion is to utilize exercises that stimulate active discussion of diverse alternatives without threatening the group and intensifying identity protection. One such exercise is to have group members talk about dangers or risks involved in a decision and delaying discussion of any potential gains. By requiring members to first focus on the negatives of a decision alternative, the group is less likely to stifle dissenting views and more likely to gain an objective evaluation.

TRUTH
47

How to Reduce
Work–Life Conflicts

The typical employee in the 1960s or 1970s showed up at the workplace Monday through Friday and did his or her job in eight- or nine-hour chunks of time. Both the workplace and hours of work were clearly specified. That's no longer true for many in today's workforce. Employees are increasingly complaining that the line between work and nonwork time has become blurred, creating personal conflicts and stress.

A number of forces have contributed to blurring the lines between employees' work life and personal life. First, the creation of global organizations means their world never sleeps. At any time and on any day, for instance, thousands of General Electric employees are working in countries throughout the world. The need to consult with colleagues or customers 8 or 10 time zones away means that many employees of global firms are "on-call" 24 hours a day. Second, communication technology allows employees to do their work at home, in their car, or on the beach in Tahiti. This lets many people in technical and professional jobs do their work any time and from any place. Third, organizations are asking employees to put in longer hours. Over a recent 10-year period, the average U.S. workweek increased from 43 to 47 hours; and the number of people working 45 or more hours a week jumped from 24 to 37 percent. Finally, fewer families have only a single breadwinner. Today's married employee is typically part of a dual-career couple, often with children at home. In 1980, about half of married women with children worked outside the home. Today, that number is more than 70 percent. This makes it increasingly difficult for married employees to find the time to fulfill commitments to home, spouse, children, parents, and friends.

Employees are increasingly recognizing that work is squeezing out personal lives, and they're not happy about it. For example, recent studies suggest that employees want jobs that give them flexibility in their work schedules so they can better manage work–life conflicts. In addition, the next generation of employees is likely to show similar

> Employees are increasingly recognizing that work is squeezing out personal lives, and they're not happy about it.

concerns. A majority of college and university students say that attaining a balance between personal life and work is a primary career goal. They want "a life" as well as a job! Managers who don't help their people achieve work–life balance will find it increasingly hard to attract and retain the most capable and motivated employees.

So, as a manager, what can you do to help your employees who are experiencing work–life conflicts? The overlying answer is: Give employees flexibility and options. The more obvious examples of options include providing employees with flexible work hours, telecommuting, paid leave time, and on-site support services like child-care and fitness centers. But other options that can make life easier for employees include job sharing, summer day camps for children, elder-care referral services, dry cleaning pick-up and delivery, on-site car maintenance, help in finding jobs for spouses and partners, and free income tax and legal information advisory services.

Many high-tech firms are setting the pace in helping employees balance work–life obligations. For instance, Intel has opened satellite offices around the San Francisco Bay area to accommodate employees who don't want to come into the head office. Cisco Systems has opened a $10 million child-care center that can accommodate up to 440 children. Microsoft offers free grocery delivery. Qualcomm has on-site fitness centers. And Google has free doctors on site and gives new parents up to $500 for take-out meals during the first four weeks that they are home with a new baby.

> Managers who don't help their people achieve work–life balance will find it increasingly hard to attract and retain the most capable and motivated employees.

TRUTH

48

Negotiating Isn't About Winning and Losing

Negotiations are about winning and losing, right? Wrong.

Negotiation is one of the most useful and powerful management tools for reaching agreements on a wide variety of issues—from work goals to pay raises to team assignments. But the process is not about one side winning. It's about seeking a solution in which both sides feel satisfied. Think win-win rather than win-lose. That is, seek solutions in which both you and your opponent can feel victorious rather than zero-sum outcomes, where your gains come at your opponent's expense.

Successful negotiations begin with careful planning. Acquire as much information as you can about your opponent's interests and goals. What are this person's real needs versus wants?

Think win-win rather than win-lose.

What constituencies must your opponent appease? What is this person's strategy? What is your best estimate of your opponent's objective? How entrenched is he or she in achieving that objective? What might be the least he or she would consider as an acceptable outcome? This information will help you understand your opponent's behavior, predict responses to your offers, and frame solutions in terms of his or her interests.

Next, create your own strategy. How strong is your situation, and how important is the issue? Are you willing to split differences to achieve an early solution? What is the minimal outcome you are willing to accept? Like a good chess player, think ahead to what actions your opponent might take; then set up an effective response to each.

Begin the actual negotiations with a positive overture—perhaps a small concession. Studies show that concessions tend to be reciprocated and lead to agreements. A positive climate can be further developed by reciprocating your opponent's concessions. And don't be shy about making the first offer. Creating an initial offer provides an opportunity to demonstrate good intent and open the discussion. Contrary to what many believe, starting first favors the person starting, not the other way around.

Address problems, not personalities. Concentrate on the negotiation issues, not on the personal characteristics of your opponent. Avoid being confrontational or attacking your opponent. If other people feel threatened, they concentrate on defending their self-esteem as opposed to solving the problem. It's your opponent's ideas or position that you disagree with, not the person. Separate the people from the problem and don't personalize differences.

Try to maintain a rational, goal-oriented frame of mind. Don't get hooked by emotional outbursts. Let the other person blow off steam without taking it personally.

Address problems, not personalities.

While it is in your best interests to initiate an offer, treat your opponent's initial offer as merely a point of departure. Don't give it a lot of attention. Initial offers tend to be extreme and idealistic.

Emphasize win-win solutions. They build long-term relationships and facilitate working together in the future. For instance, consider creating additional alternatives, especially low-cost concessions you can make that have high value to your opponent. Frame options in terms of your opponent' interests, and look for solutions that can allow both of you to declare a victory.

TRUTH

49

Not Everyone Wants a Challenging Job

Does everyone want a challenging job? In spite of all the attention focused by the media, academicians, and social scientists on human potential and the needs of individuals, there is no evidence to support that the vast majority of workers want challenging jobs. Some individuals prefer highly complex and challenging jobs; others prosper in simple, routine work.

The individual-difference variable that seems to gain the greatest support for explaining who prefers a challenging job and who doesn't is the strength of an individual's needs for personal growth and self-direction at work. Individuals with these higher-order growth needs are more responsive to challenging work. What percentage of rank-and-file workers actually desire higher-order need satisfactions and will respond positively to challenging jobs? No current data is available, but a study from the 1970s estimated the figure at about 15 percent. Even after adjusting for changing work attitudes and the growth in white-collar jobs, it seems unlikely that the number today exceeds 40 percent.

The strongest voice advocating challenging jobs has *not* been workers; it's been professors, social science researchers, and media people. Professors, researchers, and journalists undoubtedly made their career choices, to some degree, because they wanted jobs that gave them autonomy, recognition, and challenge. That, of course, is their choice. But for them to project their needs onto the workforce in general is presumptuous. Not every employee is looking for a challenging job. Many workers meet their higher-order needs *off* the job. There are 168 hours in every individual's week. Work rarely consumes more than 30 percent of this time. That leaves considerable opportunity, even for individuals with strong growth needs, to find higher-order need satisfaction outside the workplace.

> Many workers meet their higher-order needs off the job.

What's the message here for managers? Don't feel you have a responsibility to create challenging jobs for *all* your employees. For many people, work is something that will never excite or challenge them. And they don't expect to find their growth opportunities at work. Work is merely something they have to do to pay their bills. They can find challenges outside work on the golf course, fishing, at their local pub, with their friends in social clubs, with their family, and the like.

For many people, work is something that will never excite or challenge them.

TRUTH

50

Four Job-Design Actions That Will Make Employees More Productive

In spite of the reality that there are no ideal job designs that are right for everyone, there is substantial evidence that many people seem to have four common characteristics they prefer in a job. To the degree that you enrich jobs in your firm by encompassing these characteristics, you increase the probability that people will like their jobs and be motivated to generate high productivity in those jobs.

The following suggestions specify the types of changes in jobs that are most likely to lead to improving their productivity potential.

1. **Combine tasks.** Managers should seek to take existing and fractionalized tasks and put them together to form a new and larger module of work. This allows employees to do a greater variety of tasks, display more of their talent and skills, and form an identifiable and meaningful whole. It also increases employee "ownership" of the work and improves the likelihood that employees will view their work as meaningful and important. To illustrate, at the Corning Glass Works plant in Medford, Massachusetts, work tasks were combined to make jobs more interesting. Employees who previously worked on only a single part that went into laboratory hot plates now put entire hot-plate units together.

> Managers should seek to take existing and fractionalized tasks and put them together.

2. **Establish client relationships.** The client is the user of the product or service that the employee works on (and may be an "internal customer" as well as someone outside the organization). Wherever possible, you should try to establish direct relationships between workers and their clients. This makes the job more interesting and diverse, allows the employee to get direct customer feedback on his or her performance, and gives the employee a greater feeling of ownership over his or her work. At John Deere, some assembly-line workers have been included as part of the sales teams that call on customers. These workers know the products

better than any traditional salesperson, and by traveling and speaking with farmers, these hourly workers develop a better understanding of the customers' needs. They also now feel more involved in their jobs because they know what happens to the tractors and machinery they build once it leaves the factory.

3. **Expand jobs vertically.** Vertical expansion gives employees responsibilities and control that were formerly reserved for management. It seeks to partially close the gap between the "doing" and the "controlling" aspects of the job, and it increases employee autonomy.

The use of self-managed teams has been effective in increasing verticality. At the L-S Electrogalvanizing Co., in Cleveland, Ohio, the entire plant is run by self-managed teams, doing many of the tasks that used to be reserved for management. The teams do their own hiring and scheduling, rotate jobs on their own, establish production targets, set pay scales that are linked to skills, and fire coworkers.

> Vertical expansion of jobs gives employees responsibilities and control that were formerly reserved for management.

4. **Open feedback channels.** When managers increase feedback, employees not only learn how well they are performing their jobs, but also whether their performance is improving, deteriorating, or remaining at a constant level. Ideally, this feedback about performance should be received directly as the employee does the job, rather than from management on an occasional basis. Mechanics at General Electric's aircraft engine plant in Durham, North Carolina, get immediate feedback on how they're performing. The plant is designed around self-managed teams, and the team members take on responsibility for providing ongoing feedback to each other so the team can continually improve its performance.

TRUTH

51

Annual Reviews: The Best Surprise Is No Surprise!

A number of years ago, Holiday Inn built an advertising campaign around the slogan, "The best surprise is NO surprise!" That slogan would also make good advice today to managers when it comes to giving annual performance reviews.

Few managers enjoy giving performance reviews. Why? There seems to be at least three reasons.

First, managers are often uncomfortable discussing performance weaknesses directly with employees. Given that almost every employee could stand to improve in some areas, managers fear a confrontation when presenting negative feedback. This apparently even applies when people give negative feedback to a computer! Bill Gates reported that Microsoft conducted a project that required users to rate their experience with a computer. "When we had the computer the users had worked with ask for an evaluation of its performance, the responses tended to be positive. But when we had a second computer ask the same people to evaluate their encounters with the first machine, the people were significantly more critical. Their reluctance to criticize the first computer 'to its face' suggested that they didn't want to hurt its feelings, even though they knew it was only a machine."

> Managers are often uncomfortable discussing performance weaknesses directly with employees.

Second, many employees tend to become defensive when their weaknesses are pointed out. Instead of accepting the feedback as constructive and a basis for improving performance, some employees challenge the evaluation by criticizing the manager or redirecting blame to someone else. A survey of 151 area managers in Philadelphia, for instance, found that 98 percent of these managers encountered some type of aggression after giving employees negative appraisals.

Finally, employees tend to have an inflated assessment of their own performance. Statistically speaking, half of all employees must be below-average performers. But the evidence indicates that the average employee's estimate of his or her own performance level generally falls around the 75th percentile. So even when managers are providing good news, employees are likely to perceive it as not good enough!

Employees tend to have an inflated assessment of their own performance.

The solution to the performance feedback problem is two-fold. First, performance feedback shouldn't be avoided. To the contrary, it needs to be continuous. Don't save up your assessments and then spring them on an employee in his or her annual review. You should be providing feedback all the time. And when the formal review *is* held, the employee shouldn't be confronted with any surprises. The formal annual review should be an aggregate summary of what the employee has been hearing all year long. Providing continuous feedback is especially important for Generation Y. As we noted in Truth 17, "Managing Across the Generation Gap," this group prefers frequent performance feedback. For instance, in a survey of employees at Ernst & Young, 85 percent of Gen Y's said their age-group peers wanted frequent and candid performance feedback, whereas only half of Baby Boomers agreed.

Second, all managers need to be trained in how to conduct constructive feedback sessions. An effective review—one in which the employee perceives the appraisal as fair, the manager as sincere, and the climate as constructive—can result in the employee leaving the interview in an upbeat mood, informed about the performance areas in which he or she needs to improve, and determined to correct the deficiencies.

TRUTH

52

Don't Blame Me! The Role of Self-Serving Bias

Did you ever notice that people are pretty good at deflecting blame for failures yet they're quick to take credit for successes? This is not a random occurrence. In fact, it's predictable.

Our perceptions of people differ from our perceptions of inanimate objects such as machines or buildings because we make inferences about the actions of people that we don't make about inanimate objects. The result is that when we observe people, we attempt to develop explanations of why they behave in certain ways. Our perception and judgment of a person's actions, therefore, will be significantly influenced by the assumptions we make about that person's internal state.

Attribution theory can help us explain the ways in which we judge people differently, depending on what meaning we attribute to a given behavior. Basically, when we observe an individual's behavior, we attempt to determine whether it was internally or externally caused. That determination, however, depends largely on three factors: (1) distinctiveness, (2) consensus, and (3) consistency. First, let's clarify the differences between internal and external causation, and then we'll elaborate on each of the three determining factors.

Internally caused behaviors are those that are believed to be under the personal control of the individual. *Externally* caused behavior is seen as resulting from outside causes; that is, the person is seen as having been forced into the behavior by the situation. If one of your employees is late for work, you

> We judge people differently, depending on what meaning we attribute to a given behavior.

might attribute his lateness to his partying into the wee hours of the morning and then oversleeping. This would be an internal attribution. But if you attribute his arriving late to a major automobile accident that tied up traffic on the road that this employee regularly uses, then you would be making an external attribution.

Distinctiveness refers to whether an individual displays different behaviors in different situations. Is the employee who arrives late today also the source of complaints by coworkers for being a "goof-off"? What we want to know is whether this behavior is unusual. If it is, the observer is likely to give the behavior an external attribution. If this action is not unusual, it will probably be judged as internal.

If everyone who is faced with a similar situation responds in the same way, we can say the behavior shows *consensus*. Our late employee's behavior would meet this criterion if all employees who took the same route to work were also late. From an attribution perspective, if consensus is high, you would be expected to give an external attribution to the employee's tardiness, whereas if other employees who took the same route made it to work on time, your conclusion as to causation would be internal.

Finally, an observer looks for *consistency* in a person's actions. Does the person respond the same way over time? Coming in 10 minutes late for work is not perceived in the same way for the employee for whom it is an unusual case (she hasn't been late for several months) as it is for the employee for whom it is part of a routine pattern (she is regularly late two or three times a week). The more consistent the behavior, the more the observer is inclined to attribute it to internal causes.

One of the more interesting findings from attribution theory is that there are errors or biases that distort attributions. For instance, there is a tendency for individuals to attribute their own successes to internal factors, such as ability or effort, while putting the blame for failure on external factors, such as luck. This self-serving bias can often make it hard to provide employees with honest and accurate feedback on their performance. Feedback given to employees in performance reviews will be predictably distorted by recipients, depending on whether it is positive or negative. So don't be surprised that employees bend over backward patting themselves on the back for a positive evaluation while looking for external factors to put the blame on when evaluations are negative.

> There is a tendency for individuals to attribute their own successes to internal factors, such as ability or effort, while putting the blame for failure on external factors, such as luck.

TRUTH
53

Judging Others:
Tips for Making Better
Decisions

The performance-review process requires a large component of decision making. We've learned over the years that making decision judgments is fraught with biases. Here, we want to alert you to several additional judgmental distortions that we're all vulnerable to and offer some advice on how you can minimize those distortions.

Overconfidence bias. When we're given factual questions and asked to judge the probability that our answers are correct, we tend to be far too optimistic. For instance, studies have found that when people say they're 65 to 70 percent confident that they're right, they were actually correct only about 50 percent of the time. And when they say they're 100 percent sure, they tended to be 70 to 85 percent correct.

> Decision judgments are fraught with biases.

When we are doing performance evaluations, this optimistic bias tends to make us overconfident in the accuracy of our appraisals. So what can you do? Begin by recognizing that you're likely to be overconfident. Also, search hard for disconfirming evidence and look for reasons why your assessment might be wrong. Input from others (see Truth 54, "The Case for 360-Degree Feedback Appraisals: More IS Better,") also helps to limit this bias.

Availability bias. We have a tendency to base our judgments on information that is readily available. Events that evoke emotions, that are particularly vivid, or that have occurred more recently tend to be more available in our memory. This bias explains why managers, when doing performance appraisals, tend to give more weight to recent employee behaviors than those behaviors of six or nine months ago.

We offer two suggestions for countering this bias. First, don't rely on your memory. Keep a journal for each of your employees on his or her job performance and update it regularly. Second, question your data. Ask yourself: Am I being unduly influenced by information that is readily available, recent, or vivid?

Selective perception bias. Any characteristic that makes a person stand out will increase the probability that the characteristic will be perceived. Why? Because it is impossible for us to assimilate everything we see; only certain stimuli can be taken in. This tendency explains why some employees will be reprimanded by their boss for doing something that, when done by another employee, goes unnoticed. Because we can't observe everything going on about us, we engage in selective perception. This allows us to "speed-read" others but not without the risk of drawing an inaccurate picture.

We can't eliminate selective perception. Each of us brings to every situation the baggage of our past experiences, attitudes, and vested interests. We can, however, actively attempt to minimize our perceptual biases by acknowledging that there is no pure objectivity and that both "truth and beauty are in the eye of the beholder"; trying to understand our perceptual biases by assessing what expectation we bring to a situation that might cloud the way we see it; and asking ourselves whether someone else with different expectations might see the same situation differently.

Confirmation bias. This is actually just a specific case of selective perception but, nonetheless, a common problem in performance appraisals. It says that we seek out information that reaffirms our past choices and we discount information that contradicts past judgments. We also tend to accept at face value any information that confirms our preconceived views, while being critical and skeptical of information that challenges these views. In performance appraisals, when we like someone, we look for information that confirms that belief. When we don't like someone, we do the opposite.

> We seek out information that reaffirms our past choices, and we discount information that contradicts past judgments.

The confirmation bias is hard to overcome. The obvious solution—to aggressively search out contrary or disconfirming information—has been found to be difficult for people to actually do. The best advice is to be honest about your motives. Are you seriously trying to get information in order to make an informed decision, or are you just looking for evidence to confirm what you'd like to do? You need to purposely seek out disconfirming information, which means you need to be prepared to hear what you don't want to hear. You also need to practice skepticism until it becomes habitual. You have to train yourself to consistently challenge your favored beliefs.

54

The Case for 360-Degree Feedback Appraisals: More IS Better!

Employees at the Cook Children's Health Care System in Fort Worth, Texas, aren't evaluated only by their supervisor. They also get evaluated by patients, coworkers, and people in other departments who interact with them. The reason is that Cook has implemented 360-degree performance appraisal. It's intended to provide more accurate and diverse input on an employee's performance by seeking feedback from varied sources such as bosses, peers, subordinates, team members, customers, and suppliers. Its popularity is reflected by the fact that nearly 90 percent of Fortune 1000 firms now use this approach for their employee appraisals.

The 360-degree feedback system recognizes that performance varies across contexts and that individuals behave differently with different constituencies. When you get feedback from various constituencies, the reliability of the performance evaluation is increased. So, 360-degree appraisals capture the reality that an employee's performance typically is made up of multiple behaviors and that access to observing those different behaviors varies among constituencies. Multiple evaluations by different constituencies have been found to capture this variety of behavior and improve the quality of the performance appraisal data.

Nearly 90 percent of Fortune 1000 firms now use this approach for their employee appraisals.

In the typical 360-degree appraisal system, employees are evaluated by 8 to 12 people. Ideally, they should be individuals who work closely with the employee and have direct contact in assessing his or her performance. It's been found that 360-degree feedback works best with employees who work in teams or at a distance from their bosses. In the former case, team members are better able to accurately assess an employee's contribution than his or her immediate supervisor. In the latter case, remote bosses often have little day-to-day contact with the employee, and evaluations tend to be inaccurate because they're based on limited and selected bits of information. In the case of a sales representative who is on the road most of the time, the customers he or she meets with regularly can offer performance insights that a supervisor would never be privy to.

Jay Marshall found 360-degree feedback helpful when he was a partner at Booz Allen. In charge of a team of about 75 consultants, Marshall learned through a 360-degree review that he had "become invisible" to the consultants he was overseeing. The feedback he got made him realize that he was spending too much time trying to keep the client happy and shortchanging his team of the time they needed from him. That feedback wouldn't have been possible from his boss or other superiors who never visited his job site.

When you get feedback from various constituencies, the reliability of the performance evaluation is increased.

The major problem you need to be aware of with these appraisals is the tendency of evaluators to use them as a means of "getting even" with an employee. This can be particularly troublesome with input provided by subordinates and peers. Since reviews are usually anonymous, evaluators with an axe to grind can use the system to even scores. To help alleviate this problem, most companies allow employees to choose which subordinates and peers they want to review them. While this can create a tendency for individuals to selectively "choose friends," this bias can be reduced by ensuring that a substantial number of evaluations are sought. A sample of only 3 or 4 evaluations can be easily manipulated. But a sample of 10 or 12 is likely to provide a reasonably accurate picture of the evaluatee's strengths and weaknesses.

TRUTH

55

Most People Resist Any Change That Doesn't Jingle in Their Pockets!

One of the most well-documented findings from studies of organizational behavior is that organizations and their members resist change. In one sense, this is positive. It provides a degree of stability and predictability to behavior. If there weren't some resistance, organizational behavior would take on characteristics of chaotic randomness. Resistance to change can also be a source of functional conflict. For example, resistance to a reorganization plan or a change in a product line can stimulate a healthy debate over the merits of the idea and result in a better decision. But there is a definite downside to resistance to change. It hinders adaptation and progress.

Resistance to change doesn't necessarily surface in standardized ways. Resistance can be overt, implicit, immediate, or deferred. It's easiest for management to deal with resistance when it is overt and immediate. For instance, a change is proposed and employees quickly respond by voicing complaints, engaging in a work slowdown, threatening to go on strike, or the

Resistance to change hinders adaptation and progress.

like. The greater challenge is managing resistance that is implicit or deferred. Implicit resistance efforts are more subtle—loss of loyalty to the organization, loss of motivation to work, increased errors or mistakes, increased absenteeism due to "sickness"—and hence more difficult to recognize. Similarly, deferred actions cloud the link between the source of the resistance and the reaction to it. A change may produce what appears to be only a minimal reaction at the time it is initiated, but then resistance surfaces weeks, months, or even years later. Or a single change that in and of itself might have little impact becomes the straw that breaks the camel's back.

Resistance to change can come from either the individual or the organization. Let me start by highlighting some individual sources of resistance to change: habit, security, economic factors, and fear of the unknown.

We're all creatures of *habit*. Life is complex enough; we don't need to consider the full range of options for the hundreds of decisions we have to make every day. To cope with this complexity, we all rely on habits or programmed responses. But when we are confronted with change, this tendency to respond in our accustomed ways becomes a source of resistance. People with a high need for *security* are likely to resist change because it threatens their feelings of safety. Another source of individual resistance is concern that changes will lower one's income. Changes in job tasks or established work routines also can arouse *economic* fears if people are concerned that they won't be able to perform the new tasks or routines to their previous standards, especially when pay is closely tied to productivity. Changes substitute ambiguity and uncertainty for the known. You trade the known for the *unknown* and the fear or insecurity that goes with it.

Organizations, by their very nature, are conservative. They actively resist change through structural and group inertia, and threats to member expertise, power relationships, and established resource allocations.

Organizations have built-in mechanisms to produce stability. For example, the selection process systematically selects certain people in and certain people out. Training reinforces specific role requirements and skills. Formalization provides job descriptions, rules, and procedures for employees to follow. When an organization is confronted with change, *this structural inertia* acts as a counterbalance to sustain stability. And even if individuals want to change their behavior, group norms

> Organizations have built-in mechanisms to produce stability.

may act as a constraint. Changes in organizational patterns may threaten the expertise of specialized groups and long-established power relationships within the organization. For instance, those groups in the organization that control sizable resources often see change as a threat. They tend to be content with the way things are.

What does all this mean to you as a manager? First, initiating change is an important part of most managers' jobs. Second, expect resistance to change to come in a number of forms. And finally, be prepared to undermine this resistance by providing rewards for accepting change, communicating reasons for why a change is necessary, and including people who will be affected by the change to participate in change decisions.

TRUTH

56

Use Participation to Reduce Resistance to Change

It had been a year since John Rose had opened his Rose Bud Bakery and Café—and business was booming. In 12 short months, he had outgrown the 1,200 square feet he had originally rented. So he negotiated to take over an additional 1,000 square feet next door. Then, in what many of his business friends thought was a bit strange, he closed Rose Bud for an entire day one Wednesday but paid his staff of 11 people to still come in. Starting at 8 a.m., John laid out his problem—the business was dramatically short of space—and his solution of renting additional space. But then he said, "You know as much about this business and our needs as I do. I want to spend this day getting your input on a number of issues—for instance: Where's the best place to relocate the kitchen? How can we design the new space to move customers through as efficiently as possible? How much space should we allocate to the display counters and how much to seating? What, if any, new offerings should we consider? How can we combine the two spaces with the least disturbance to our normal operations? When would be the best time to make the move?"

As John expected, he got some terrific feedback from his staff. And Sherry Meyer, one of John's kitchen staff, summarized the feeling of most of the employees: "I really appreciate that John wanted our input. I now understand what's going on, and I'm 100 percent behind him."

Having employees participate in decisions that affect them is no panacea. Participation has only a modest influence on factors such as employee productivity, motivation, and job satisfaction. But, as John Rose understood, it's a potent force for combating resistance to change. For instance, a study of 300 middle managers at an Italian electric utility found that participation in the development and implementation of a change initiative resulted in more positive attitudes toward the change and reduced resistance to change. Similarly, a study of 138 managers at a large telecommunications company that was going through a major strategic reorientation found a strong relationship between employee perceptions of their participation and reduced resistance.

It's difficult for individuals to resist a change decision in which they participated. So prior to making a change, consider whether the conditions are right for using participation. What are those conditions? First, there must be adequate time to participate. Many decisions in organizations must be made quickly, with little lead time. Such decisions don't lend themselves to employee participation. Second, the issues in which the employees are asked to get involved

It's difficult for individuals to resist a change decision in which they participated.

in must be relevant to their interests. They should be related to the employee's job, his or her welfare, or have a clear link to something that the employee is interested in. Third, the employees must have the ability to participate. This includes the intelligence, technical knowledge, and communication skills to contribute to the decision process. Finally, the organization's culture must support employee involvement. Employees aren't likely to take participation efforts seriously when the company's culture has long been dominated by autocratic decision making and ignoring employee input.

When the preceding four conditions exist, participation can reduce resistance, obtain commitment, and increase the quality of the change decision. And companies have found varied ways of bringing employees into decisions that involve change. Suggestion programs, for instance, identify and reward employees who offer ideas for change. Quality circles provide opportunities for groups of employees, in shared areas of responsibility, to discuss their quality problems, investigate causes of those problems, and recommend solutions to management. Many firms are adding employee representatives to executive task forces designed to address major changes. And an increasing number of North American companies

Participation can reduce resistance, obtain commitment, and increase the quality of the change decision.

are adopting the popular Western European approach of including employee representatives on their board of directors.

TRUTH

57

Employee Turnover Can Be a Good Thing

The traditional view of voluntary turnover is that it has a negative impact on organizational performance. When an employee quits and has to be replaced, an organization incurs both obvious and hidden costs. They include the costs of recruiting, selecting, and training new hires; as well as the additional inefficiencies from workflow disruptions as new employees learn their job, make mistakes, and "get up to speed" in understanding the organization's culture.

While this traditional view is intuitively appealing, it's a gross generalization. The evidence suggests that low levels of turnover can be functional, especially in certain organizations or departments within organizations.

Why can turnover be functional? Let me offer at least three reasons. First, turnover clears out low producers. When management obsessively strives for minimal turnover, it lessens the likelihood of identifying and removing low-performing employees. When low producers are removed, the organization's overall level of performance improves. Second, turnover increases promotional opportunities. New rungs on the corporate ladder open up opportunities for those employees who stay. And third, turnover can increase functional conflict, which, in turn, increases workforce innovation, flexibility, and adaptability. It supplies fresh ideas and perspectives. Turnover can be particularly valuable at stimulating stagnant or entrenched teams.

Turnover can also benefit an organization by keeping down employee labor costs. In a large number of jobs, wages tend to increase over time, but there is no comparable increase in productivity. Employees get annual raises, their salaries continue to grow each year, but their contribution is essentially unchanged. It's not unusual, for instance, for an employee with 15 years of service to be earning 50 to 100 percent more than his or her counterpart with 2 years of service—the difference in pay due solely to length of tenure in the organization. Additionally, given that employee benefits tend to

> Turnover can benefit an organization by keeping down employee labor costs.

be a percentage of direct labor costs, these too go up as employee seniority increases. As a case in point, a new employee may get only 2 weeks annual vacation while a senior counterpart gets 5 weeks.

Do any organizations pursue a functional-turnover strategy? Absolutely. They include major companies like General Electric, Microsoft, Sun Microsystems, Sprint, and the Big Four accounting firms. GE, for instance, annually ranks managers and professional employees in every division and fires those in the bottom 10 percent. This approach, in turn, encourages marginal performers to leave voluntarily before they're fired. And the Big Four accounting firms report wanting to keep the performance bar high by maintaining a turnover rate of 10 to 12 percent.

The argument in favor of voluntary turnover comes with some qualifications. There is, for instance, no evidence to support that very high levels of turnover, across an organization, are beneficial. The benefits of turnover are at low-to-moderate levels. Moreover, low-to-moderate levels of turnover are more likely to be functional in jobs or organizations that rely on knowledge workers. High-tech companies, for instance, rely heavily on ideas and innovation to flourish. A lack of employee turnover in such organizations can lead to stagnation and apathy. Similarly, departments like marketing, research, and product development are dependent on fresh perspectives to maintain their viability. In contrast, employee turnover is likely to be almost entirely dysfunctional in jobs and organizations that rely heavily on minimum-wage workers.

> Turnover can be functional, especially when the right people are turning over.

Our conclusion is that managers should not automatically assume that vigorous action to minimize any employee turnover is in the organization's best interests. In many cases, turnover can be functional, especially when the right people are turning over.

58

In Cutbacks: Don't Neglect the Survivors

The last decade has seen a number of major organizations reducing their number of employees. In 2011 alone, organizations as varied as Corning, Best Buy, Goldman Sachs, Pfizer, Lockheed Martin, and the U.S. Postal System all announced massive layoffs.

When layoff announcements are made, attention naturally flows to those individuals who've lost their jobs. We expect that they're likely to suffer from depression, anxiety, and similar negative feelings. And organizations respond by offering layoff victims outplacement services, psychological counseling, support groups, and extended benefit programs. While we certainly don't want to minimize the trauma that layoffs create for those who have lost their jobs, managers often ignore the impact that downsizing has on the survivors. There is an increasing amount of evidence that indicates that layoffs have severe effects on those employees who remain after layoffs. And managers who ignore these effects and fail to address them are likely to suffer serious drops in their organization's performance.

> Managers often ignore the impact that downsizing has on the survivors.

The evidence shows both victims and survivors experience similar feelings of frustration, anxiety, and loss. But layoff victims get to move on and start over with a clean slate. This isn't true of survivors. They're likely to suffer from layoff survivor sickness. Symptoms of this sickness include job insecurity, perceptions of unfairness, depression, stress from increased workloads, fear of change, loss of loyalty and commitment, reduced risk taking and motivation, unwillingness to do anything beyond the required minimum, feelings of not being kept well informed, and a loss of confidence in upper management.

> The evidence shows both victims and survivors experience similar feelings of frustration, anxiety, and loss.

What can managers do to deal with layoff survivor sickness? A four-step approach has been suggested:

Step 1: Get the process right. Well-designed layoff processes won't cure survivor sickness, but they keep survivors from sinking deeper into survivor symptoms. Characteristics of a well-designed process include: Make the cuts clear and quick. Provide abundant information to both victims and survivors. Give layoff victims adequate prior notification. Be emotionally honest and authentic in all communications. Explain decisions openly and in terms of fairness. And, if possible, allow employees to participate.

Step 2: Let people grieve to deal with repressed feelings and emotions. Even in the best-handled layoffs, survivors feel violated. They must release their feelings before they can go on. They need to go through the same grieving process that one goes through after a death in the family. Use of groups is one of the most effective and efficient means of bringing survivor emotions to the surface. In a relatively short time, most natural work teams can make a great deal of progress in unblocking and addressing their survivor feelings.

Step 3: Break the chain of organizational dependence. This step tries to help survivors recapture their sense of control and self-esteem. While Steps 1 and 2 react to existing layoff survivor symptoms, this step offers the possibility of preventing the sickness in the first place by moving people from organizational dependency to self-directed careers. Today's workplace requires employees to build transferable skills and have independence from their employers. An employee's loyalty is no longer to the organization but to his or her own career. The breaking of this dependency relationship is essentially an individual effort.

Step 4: Reshape the organization's systems to lessen processes that create dependency. This final step seeks to help people immunize themselves against survivor sickness. Organizations historically did a lot to create dependency: Seniority systems for promotions and rewards; loyalty expectations; promotion from within; long-term socialization processes to shape people into "desired employees"; long-term career-planning; and nontransferable corporate pension plans. Organizations have to detach themselves from these paternalistic practices.

59

Beware of the Quick Fix

Too many modern managers are like compulsive dieters. They try the latest management craze for a few days (or months) and then move restlessly on to the next craze. The sad news for managers is the same that we'd offer dieters: There is no quick fix!

That said, there is no shortage of consultants, management-development professionals, and business journalists ready to pitch instant solutions to complex management problems. They've been doing it for more than five decades. In the 1960s, the list of "instant panaceas" included MBO, Theory Y management, sensitivity training, job enrichment, PERT, and the BCG Matrix. In the 1970s, you had centralized strategic planning, matrix organization designs, management by committee, flextime, and zero-base budgeting. The 1980s gave us intrapreneurship, quality circles, Theory Z, just-in-time inventory systems, Deming's 14 principles, self-managed teams, and skunk works. The 1990s offered up strategic alliances, exploiting core competencies, TQM, reengineering, mass customization, benchmarking, charismatic leadership, visionary leadership, emotional intelligence, network organizations, learning organizations, open-book management, self-managed careers, outsourcing, empowerment, and 24/7 work environments. Into the new century, we've already been told about the virtues of work-family balance, social capital, employee engagement, e-leadership, virtual organizations, customer segmentation, knowledge management, workplace spirituality, and power napping.

Managers, like all people, are susceptible to fads.

Managers, like all people, are susceptible to fads. My message here is merely to warn managers: Buyer beware!

Someone will always be selling the latest management technique. And unfortunately, rather than presenting them in a contingency framework, with recognition that these techniques work best under certain circumstances and are likely to be ineffective in other circumstances, advocates have tended to offer them as universal solutions. At the extreme, it can drive managers to run from one quick fix to another. This was driven home when a frustrated executive recently told me, "In the past couple of years, we've heard that profit is more important than revenue, that quality is more important than profit, that our people are more important than quality, that customers are more important than our people, that big customers are more important than small customers, and that growth is the key to our success."

The common theme among these "quick fixes," like diet books, is that they're sold as universal solutions to complex problems. They're rarely presented in a situational or contingency perspective. And that's the mistake. Each, in its own way, has something to offer managers. These techniques are tools in a tool chest. But just as a carpenter can't solve every problem with a hammer, managers can't solve every problem with self-managed teams or TQM. There are no shortcuts to the complex job of managing. You need to treat new ideas and concepts as additional tools that can help you be more effective in your job. But no single new idea can make a mediocre manager excellent or lead to turning around a poorly managed organization.

No single new idea can make a mediocre manager excellent or lead to turning around a poorly managed organization.

References

Truth 1

Bardack, N.R., and F.T. McAndrew, "The Influence of Physical Attractiveness and Manner of Dress on Success in a Simulated Personnel Decision," *Journal of Social Psychology* (August 1985): 777–78.

Dougherty, T.W., D.B. Turban, and J.C. Callender, "Confirming First Impressions in the Employment Interview: A Field Study of Interviewer Behavior," *Journal of Applied Psychology* (October 1994): 659–65.

London, M., and M.D. Hakel, "Effects of Applicant Stereotypes, Order, and Information on Interview Impressions," *Journal of Applied Psychology* (April 1974): 157–62.

Macan, T.M., and R.L. Dipboye, "The Relationship of the Interviewers' Preinterview Impressions to Selection and Recruitment Outcomes," *Personnel Psychology* (Autumn 1990): 745–69.

Truth 2

Davis-Blake, A., and J. Pfeffer, "Just a Mirage: The Search for Dispositional Effects in Organizational Research," *Academy of Management Review* (July 1989): 385–400.

Mischel, W., "The Interaction of Person and Situation," in D. Magnusson and N.S. Endler (eds.), *Personality at the Crossroads: Current Issues in Interactional Psychology*. Hillsdale, NJ: Earlbaum Associates, 1977: 333–52.

Truth 3

Byington, E., and W. Felps, "Why Do IQ Scores Predict Job Performance? An Alternative, Sociological Explanation," in R.M. Kramer and B.M. Staw (eds.), *Research in Organizational Behavior*, vol. 30. Oxford: Elsevier, 2010: 175–202.

Le, H., I-S Oh, J. Shaffer, and F. Schmidt, "Implications of Methodological Advances for the Practice of Personnel Selection: How Practitioners Benefit from Meta-Analysis," *Academy of Management Perspectives* (August 2007): 6–15.

Ree, M.J., J.A. Earles, and M.S. Teachout, "Predicting Job Performance: Not Much More Than g," *Journal of Applied Psychology* (August 1994): 518–24.

Ree, M.J., T.R. Carretta, and J.R. Steindl, "Cognitive Ability," in N. Anderson, D.S. Ones, H.K. Sinangil, and C. Viswesvaran (eds.), *Handbook of Industrial Work & Organizational Psychology,* vol. 1. Thousand Oaks, CA: Sage, 2001: 219–32.

Schmidt, F., H Le, I-S Oh, and J. Shaffer, "General Mental Ability, Job Performance, and Red Herrings: Responses to Osterman, Hauser, and Schmitt," *Academy of Management Perspectives* (November 2007): 64–76.

Schmidt, F.L., "The Role of General Cognitive Ability in Job Performance: Why There Cannot Be a Debate," *Human Performance* (April 2002): 187–211.

Schmidt, F.L. and J.E. Hunter, "General Mental Ability in the World of Work: Occupational Attainment and Job Performance," *Journal of Personality and Social Psychology* (January 2004): 162–73.

Schmidt, F.L. and J.E. Hunter, "The Validity and Utility of Selection Methods in Personnel Psychology: Practical and Theoretical Implications of 85 Years of Research Findings," *Psychological Bulletin* (September 1998): 262–74.

Truth 4

Bakker, A.B., E. Demerouti, and L.L. Brummelhuis, "Work Engagement, Performance, and Active Learning: The Role of Conscientiousness," *Journal of Vocational Behavior* (April 2012): 555–64.

Barrick, M.R., and M.K. Mount, "Select on Conscientiousness and Emotional Stability," in E.A. Locke (ed.), *Handbook of Principles of Organizational Behavior.* Malden, MA: Blackwell, 2004: 15–28.

Hogan, J., and B. Holland, "Using Theory to Evaluate Personality and Job-Performance Relations: A Socioanalytic Perspective," *Journal of Applied Psychology* (February 2003): 100–12.

Hurtz, G.M., and J.J. Donovan, "Personality and Job Performance: The Big Five Revisited," *Journal of Applied Psychology,* December 2000, 869–79.

Le, H.,, L. Oh, S.B. Robbins, R. Ilies, E. Holland, and P. Westrick, "Too Much of a Good Thing: Curvilinear Relationships between Personality Traits and Job Performance," *Journal of Applied Psychology* (January 2011): 113–33.

Raymark, P.H., M.J. Schmit, and R.M. Guion, "Identifying Potentially Useful Personality Constructs for Employee Selection," *Personnel Psychology* (Autumn 1997): 723–36.

Salgado, J.F., "The Five Factor Model of Personality and Job Performance in the European Community," *Journal of Applied Psychology* (February 1997): 30–43.

Truth 5

Arvey, R.D., B.P. McCall, T.J. Bouchard, Jr., and P. Taubman, "Genetic Influences on Job Satisfaction and Work Values," *Personality and Individual Differences* (July 1994): 21–33.

Illies, R., R.D. Arvey, and T.J. Bouchard, "Darwinism, Behavioral Genetics, and Organizational Behavior: A Review and Agenda for Future Research," *Journal of Organizational Behavior* (March 2006): 121–41.

Lykken, D., and A. Tellegen, "Happiness Is a Stochastic Phenomenon," *Psychological Science* (May 1996): 186–89.

Nes, R.B., "Happiness in Behaviour Genetics: Findings and Implications," *Journal of Happiness Studies* (June 2010): 369–81.

Truth 6

Breaugh, J.A., "Realistic Job Previews: A Critical Appraisal and Future Research Directions," *Academy of Management Review* (October 1983): 612–19.

Buda, R. and B.H. Charnov, "Message Processing in Realistic Recruitment Practices," *Journal of Managerial Issues* (Fall 2003): 302–16.

Earnest, D.R., D.G. Allen, and R.S. Landis, "Mechanisms Linking Realistic Job Previews with Turnover: A Meta-Analytic Path Analysis," *Personnel Psychology* (Winter 2011): 865–97.

Hymowitz, C., "Immigrant Couple Use Their Survival Skills to Build Tech Success," *Wall Street Journal* (February 12, 2001): B1.

Phillips, J.M., "Effects of Realistic Job Previews on Multiple Organizational Outcomes: A Meta-Analysis," *Academy of Management Journal* (December 1998): 673–90.

Truth 7

Brough, P., G. Johnson, S. Drummond, S. Pennisi, and C. Timms, "Comparison of Cognitive Ability and Job Attitudes of Older and Younger Workers," *Equality, Diversity and Inclusion: An International Journal* (2011): vol. 30, no. 2, 105–26.

Labich, K., "The New Unemployed," *Fortune* (March 8, 1993): 43.

McMahan, S., and D. Sturz, "Implications for an Aging Workforce," *Journal of Education for Business* (September/October 2006): 50–55.

Ng, T.W.H., and D.C. Feldman, "Re-Examining the Relationship between Age and Voluntary Turnover," *Journal of Vocational Behavior* (June 2009): 283–94.

Ng, T.W.H., and D.C. Feldman, "The Relationship of Age to Ten Dimensions of Job Performance," *Journal of Applied Psychology* (March 2008): 392–423.

Posthuma, R.A., and M.A. Campion, "Age Stereotypes in the Workplace: Common Stereotypes, Moderators, and Future Research Directions," *Journal of Management* (February 2009): 155–88.

Stork, D., "Interests and Concerns of Older Workers: New Challenges for the Workplace," *Journal of Workplace Behavioral Health* (2008): vol. 23, no. 1–2, 165–78.

Truth 8

De Fruyt, F. and I. Mervielde, "RIASEC Types and Big Five Traits as Predictors of Employment Status and Nature of Employment," *Personnel Psychology* (Autumn 1999): 701–27.

Holland, J.L., and G.D. Gottfredson, "Studies of the Hexagonal Model: An Evaluation (or, The Perils of Stalking the Perfect Hexagon)," *Journal of Vocational Behavior* (April 1992): 158–70.

Holland, J.L., *Making Vocational Choices: A Theory of Vocational Personalities and Work Environments.* Odessa, FL: Psychological Assessment Resources, 1997.

Tracey, T.J., and J. Rounds, "Evaluating Holland's and Gati's Vocational-Interest Models: A Structural Meta-Analysis," *Psychological Bulletin* (March 1993): 229–46.

Van Iddekinge, C.H., D.J. Putka, and J.P. Campbell, "Reconsidering Vocational Interests for Personnel Selection: The Validity of an Interest-Based Selection Test in Relation to Job Knowledge, Job Performance, and Continuance Intentions," *Journal of Applied Psychology* (January 2011): 13–33.

Van Iddekinge, C.H., P.L. Roth, D.J. Putka, and S.E. Lanivich, "Are You Interested? A Meta-Analysis of Relations between Vocational Interests and Employee Performance and Turnover," *Journal of Applied Psychology* (November 2011): 1167–94.

Truth 9

De Cooman, R., S De Gieter, R. Pepermans, and S. Hermans, "Person-Organization Fit: Testing Socialization and Attraction-Selection-Attrition Hypotheses," *Journal of Vocational Behavior* (February 2009): 102–07.

Hoffman, B.J. and D.J. Woehr, "A Quantitiative Review of the Relationship between Person-Organization Fit and Behavioral Outcomes," *Journal of Vocational Behavior* (June 2006): 389–99.

Kristof, A.L., "Person-Organization Fit: An Integrative Review of Its Conceptualizations, Measurement, and Implications," *Personnel Psychology* (Spring 1996): 1–49.

O'Reilly, C.A. III, J. Chatman, and D.F. Caldwell, "People and Organizational Culture: A Profile Comparison Approach to Assessing Person-Organization Fit," *Academy of Management Journal* (September 1991): 487–516.

Schneider, B., D.B. Smith, S. Taylor, and J. Fleenor, "Personality and Organizations: A Test of the Homogeneity of Personality Hypothesis," *Journal of Applied Psychology* (June 1998): 462–70.

Schneider, B., H.W. Goldstein, and D.B. Smith, "The ASA Framework: An Update," *Personnel Psychology* (Winter 1995): 747–73.

Verquer, M.L., T.A. Beehr, and S.E. Wagner, "A Meta-Analysis of Relations between Person-Organization Fit and Work Attitudes," *Journal of Vocational Behavior* (June 2003): 473–89.

Truth 10

Hoffman, B.J., C.A. Blair, J.P. Maeriac, and D.J. Woehr, "Expanding the Criterion Domain? A Quantitative Review of the OCB Literature," *Journal of Applied Psychology* (March 2007): 555–66.

Konovsky, M.A., and D.W. Organ, "Dispositional and Contextual Determinants of Organizational Citizenship Behavior," *Journal of Organizational Behavior* (May 1996): 253–66.

Organ, D.W., *Organizational Citizenship Behavior: The Good Soldier Syndrome*. Lexington, MA: Lexington Books, 1988.

Podsakoff, N.P., S.W. Whiting, P.M. Podsakoff, and B.D. Blume, "Individual- and Organizational-Level Consequences of Organizational Citizenship Behaviors: A Meta-Analysis," *Journal of Applied Psychology* (January 2009): 122–41.

Podsakoff, P.M., S.B. MacKenzie, J.B. Paine, and D.G. Bachrach, "Organizational Citizenship Behaviors: A Critical Review of the Theoretical and Empirical Literature and Suggestions for Future Research," *Journal of Management* (June 2000): 543–58.

Truth 11

Allen, D.G., "Do Organizational Socialization Tactics Influence Newcomer Embeddedness and Turnover?" *Journal of Management* (April 2006): 237–56.

Kammeyer-Mueller, J.D., and C.R. Wanberg, "Unwrapping the Organizational Entry Process: Disentangling Multiple Antecedents and Their Pathways to Adjustment," *Journal of Applied Psychology* (October 2003): 779–94.

Kim, T-Y, D.M. Cable, and S-P Kim, "Socialization Tactics, Employee Proactivity, and Person-Organization Fit," *Journal of Applied Psychology* (March 2005): 232–41.

Saks, A.M., and J.A. Gruman, "Getting Newcomers Engaged: The Role of Socialization Tactics," *Journal of Managerial Psychology* (2011): vol. 26, no. 5, 383–402.

Van Maanen, J., "People Processing: Strategies of Organizational Socialization," *Organizational Dynamics* (Summer 1978): 19–36.

Truth 12

Reinharth, L. and M.A. Wahba, "Expectancy Theory as a Predictor of Work Motivation, Effort Expenditure, and Job Performance," *Academy of Management Journal* (September 1975): 502–37.

Van Eerde, W. and H. Thierry, "Vroom's Expectancy Models and Work-Related Criteria: A Meta-Analysis," *Journal of Applied Psychology* (October 1996): 575–86.

Vroom, V.H., *Work and Motivation*. New York: John Wiley, 1964.

Truth 13

Kleingeld, A., H. van Mierlo and L. Arends, "The Effect of Goal Setting on Group Performance: A Meta-Analysis," *Journal of Applied Psychology* (November 2011): 1289–304.

Locke, E.A., "Motivation Through Conscious Goal Setting," *Applied and Preventive Psychology* (1996): vol. 5, 117–24.

Locke, E.A. and G.P. Latham, *A Theory of Goal Setting and Task Performance*. Upper Saddle River, NJ: Prentice Hall, 1990.

Locke, E.A. and G.P. Latham, "Building a Practically Useful Theory of Goal Setting and Task Motivation," *American Psychologist* (September 2002): 705–17.

Wofford, J.C., V.L. Goodwin, and S. Premack, "Meta-Analysis of the Antecedents of Personal Goal Level and of the Antecedents and Consequences of Goal Commitment," *Journal of Management* (1992): vol. 18, no. 3, 595–615.

Truth 14

Collins, D., "The Ethical Superiority and Inevitability of Participatory Management as an Organizational System," *Organization Science* (September–October 1997): 489–507.

Erez, M., P.C. Earley, and C.L. Hulin, "The Impact of Participation on Goal Acceptance and Performance: A Two-Step Model," *Academy of Management Journal* (March 1985): 50–66.

Heller, F., E. Pusic, G. Strauss, and B. Wilpert, *Organizational Participation: Myth and Reality*. Oxford: Oxford University Press, 1998.

Wagner, J.A. III, "Participation's Effects on Performance and Satisfaction: A Reconsideration of Research Evidence," *Academy of Management Review* (April 1994): 312–30.

Truth 15

Baumann, N. and D. Scheffer, "Seeking Flow in the Achievement Domain: The Achievement Flow Motive Behind Flow Experience," *Motivation and Emotion* (2010): vol. 35, no. 3, 267–84.

Csikszentmihalyi, M., *Finding Flow*. New York: Basic Books, 1997.

Csikszentmihalyi, M., *Flow: The Psychology of Optimal Experience*. New York: HarperCollins, 1990.

Csikszentmihalyi, M., S. Abuhamdeh and J. Nakamura, "Flow," in A.J. Elliot and C.S. Dweck (eds.), *Handbook of Competence and Motivation*. New York: Guilford Publications, 2005: 598–608.

Truth 16

Cummings, L.L., "Appraisal Purpose and the Nature, Amount, and Frequency of Feedback," paper presented at the American Psychological Association meeting, Washington, DC, September 1976.

Ilgen, D., C.D. Fisher, and M.S. Taylor, "Consequences of Individual Feedback on Behavior in Organizations," *Journal of Applied Psychology* (August 1979): 349–71.

Mill, C.R., "Feedback: The Art of Giving and Receiving Help," in L. Porter and C.R. Mill (eds.), *The Reading Book for Human Relations Training*. Bethel: ME: NTL Institute for Applied Behavioral Science, 1976: 18–19.

Truth 17

Gibson, J.W., R.A. Greenwood and E.F. Murphy Jr., "Generational Differences in the Workplace: Personal Values, Behaviors, and Popular Beliefs," *Journal of Diversity Management* (Third Quarter 2009): 1–7.

Lockwood, N.R., F.R. Cepero, and S. Williams, *The Multigenerational Workforce*. Alexandria, VA: Society for Human Resource Management, 2009.

Lowe, D., K.J. Levitt, and T. Wilson, "Solutions for Retaining Generation Y Employees in the Workplace," *Business Renaissance Quarterly* (Fall 2008): 43–57.

Smola, K.W. and C.D. Sutton, "Generational Differences: Revisiting Generational Work Values for the New Millennium," *Journal of Organizational Behavior* (June 2002): 363–82.

Tulgan, B., *Not Everyone Gets a Trophy: How to Manage Generation Y.* San Francisco: Jossey-Bass, 2009.

Truth 18

Kerr, S., "On the Folly of Rewarding A, While Hoping for B," *Academy of Management Executive* (February 1995): 7–14.

"The Cop-Out Cops," *National Observer*, August 3, 1974.

Truth 19

Adams, J.S., "Inequity in Social Exchanges," in L. Berkowitz (ed.), *Advances in Experimental Social Psychology*. New York: Academic Press, 1965: 267–300.

Harris, M.M., F. Anseel, and F. Lievens, "Keeping Up with the Joneses: A Field Study of the Relationships among Upward, Lateral, and Downward Comparisons and Pay Level Satisfaction," *Journal of Applied Psychology* (May 2008): 665–73.

Mowday, R.T., "Equity Theory Predictions of Behavior in Organizations," in R. Steers, L.W. Porter, and G. Bigley (eds.), *Motivation and Work Behavior*, 6th ed. New York: McGraw Hill, 1996: 111–31.

Simons, T. and Q. Roberson, "Why Managers Should Care About Fairness: The Effects of Aggregate Justice Perceptions on Organizational Outcomes," *Journal of Applied Psychology* (June 2003): 432–43.

Werner, S. and N.P. Mero, "Fair or Foul? The Effects of External, Internal, and Employee Equity on Changes in Performance of Major League Baseball Players," *Human Relations* (October 1999): 1291–1312.

Truth 20

Hastings, R.R., "Recognition Practices Could Be Improved," *HRMagazine* (August 2011): 22.

Leonard, B., "The Key to Unlocking an Inexpensive Recognition Plan," *HR Magazine* (October 1999): 26.

Luthans, F. and A.D. Stajkovic, "Provide Recognition for Performance Improvement," in E.A. Locke (ed.), *Handbook of Principles of Organizational Behavior*. Maiden, MA: Blackwell, 2004: 166–80.

Nelson, B., "Try Praise," *INC.* (September 1996): 115.

Palmer, A., "Planners Are Using a Wide Range of Awards," *Incentive* (November/December 2011): 9.

Shiraz, N., M. Rashid, and A. Riza, "The Impact of Reward and Recognition Programs on Employee's Motivation and Satisfaction," *Interdisciplinary Journal of Contemporary Research in Business* (July 2011): 1428–32.

Stewart, P., "Greet Your Team with Thanks and Praise," *Firstline* (November 2011): 10–13.

Truth 21

Blumberg, M., and C.D. Pringle, "The Missing Opportunity in Organizational Research: Some Implications for a Theory of Work Performance," *Academy of Management Review* (October 1982): 560–69.

Hall, J., "Americans Know How to Be Productive If Managers Will Let Them," *Organizational Dynamics* (Winter 1994): 33–46.

Lingard, H., and V. Francis, "Does a Supportive Work Environment Moderate the Relationship between Work-Family Conflict and Burnout among Construction Professionals?" *Construction Management & Economics* (2006): vol. 24, no. 2, 185–96.

Truth 22

Andersen, J.A., "Leadership, Personality and Effectiveness," *Journal of Socio-Economics* (December 2006): 1078–91.

Arvey, R.D., M. Rotundo, W. Johnson, Z. Zhang, and M. McGue, "The Determinants of Leadership Role Occupancy: Genetic and Personality Factors," *Leadership Quarterly* (February 2006): 1–20.

Chan, S. and A.R. Brief, "When Leadership Matters and When It Does Not: A Commentary," in D.M. Messick and R.M. Kramer (eds.), *The Psychology of Leadership*. Mahwah, NJ: Erlbaum, 2005: 321–32.

Eagly, A.H., M.C. Johannesen-Schmidt, and M.L. van Engen, "Transformational, Transactional, and Laissez-Faire Leadership Styles: A Meta-Analysis Comparing Women and Men," *Psychological Bulletin* (July 2003): 569–91.

Kerr, S. and J.M. Jermier, "Substitutes for Leadership: Their Meaning and Measurement," *Organizational Behavior and Human Performance* (December 1978): 375–403.

Lord, R.G., C.L. DeVader, and G.M. Alliger, "A Meta-Analysis of the Relation between Personality Traits and Leadership Perceptions: An Application of Validity Generalization Procedures," *Journal of Applied Psychology* (August 1986): 402–10.

Mintzberg, H., *Managers Not MBAs: A Hard Look at the Soft Practice of Managing and Management Development.* San Francisco: Berrett-Koehler, 2005.

Truth 23

Bartolome, F., "Nobody Trusts the Boss Completely—Now What?," *Harvard Business Review* (March–April 1989): 135–42.

Brower, H.H., S.W. Lester, M.A. Korsgaard, and B.R. Dineen, "A Closer Look at Trust between Managers and Subordinates: Understanding the Effects of Both Trusting and Being Trusted on Subordinate Outcomes," *Journal of Management* (March 2009): 327–47.

Cunningham, J., and J. MacGregor, "Trust and the Design of Work: Complementary Constructs in Satisfaction and Performance," *Human Relations* (December 2000): 1575–91.

Dirks, K.T., and D.L. Ferrin, "Trust in Leadership: Meta-Analytic Findings and Implications for Research and Practice," *Journal of Applied Psychology* (August 2002): 611–28.

Galford, R., and A.S. Drapeau, *The Trusted Leader.* New York: Free Press, 2003.

Schindler, P.L. and C.C. Thomas, "The Structure of Interpersonal Trust in the Workplace," *Psychological Reports* (October 1993): 563–73.

Schoorman, F.D., R.C. Mayer, and J.H. Davis, "An Integrative Model of Organizational Trust: Past, Present, and Future," *Academy of Management Review* (April 2007): 344–54.

Truth 24

Fiedler, F.E., "Leadership Experience and Leadership Performance: Another Hypothesis Shot to Hell," *Organizational Behavior and Human Performance* (January 1970): 1–14.

Fiedler, F.E., "Time-Based Measures of Leadership Experience and Organizational Performance: A Review of Research and a Preliminary Model," *Leadership Quarterly* (Spring 1992): 5–23.

Quinones, M.A., J.K. Ford, and M.S. Teachout, "The Relationship between Work Experience and Job Performance: A Conceptual and Meta-Analytic Review," *Personnel Psychology* (Winter 1995): 887–910.

Truth 25

Barone, M., "A Knack for Framing," *U.S. News & World Report* (September 8, 2003): 23.

Entman, R.M., "Framing: Toward Clarification of a Fractured Paradigm," *Journal of Communication* (Autumn 1993): 51–58.

Fairhurst, G.T., and R.A. Sarr, *The Art of Framing: Managing the Language of Leadership.* San Francisco: Jossey-Bass, 1996.

Truth 26

Bezuijen, X.M., P.T. van den Berg, K. van Dam, and H. Thierry, "Pygmalion and Employee Learning: The Role of Leader Behaviors," *Journal of Management* (October 2009): 1248–67.

Eden, D., "Leadership and Expectations: Pygmalion Effects and Other Self-Fulfilling Prophecies in Organizations," *Leadership Quarterly* (Winter 1992): 271–305.

Eden, D., "Self-Fulfilling Prophecies in Organizations," in J. Greenberg (ed.), *Organizational Behavior: The State of the Science,* 2nd. ed. Mahwah, NJ: Erlbaum, 2003: 91–122.

Eden, D., and A.B. Shani, "Pygmalion Goes to Boot Camp: Expectancy, Leadership, and Trainee Performance," *Journal of Applied Psychology* (April 1982): 194–99.

Truth 27

Conger, J.A. and R.N. Kanungo (eds.), *Charismatic Leadership in Organizations.* Thousand Oaks, CA: Sage, 1998.

Howell, J.M., and P.J. Frost, "A Laboratory Study of Charismatic Leadership," *Organizational Behavior and Human Decision Processes* (April 1989): 243–69.

Towler, A.J., *The Language of Charisma: The Effects of Training on Attitudes, Behavior, and Performance.* Rice University dissertation, 2002.

Truth 28

Baines, D., "The Dark Side of Charisma," *Canadian Business* (May 22–June 4, 2006): 142–43.

Collins, J., "Level 5 Leadership: The Triumph of Humility and Fierce Resolve," *Harvard Business Review* (January 2001): 67–76.

House, R.J. and R.N. Adiya, "The Social Scientific Study of Leadership: Quo Vadis?" *Journal of Management* (June 1997): 441.

Judge, T.A., R.F. Piccolo, and T. Kosalka, "The Bright and Dark Sides of Leader Traits: A Review and Theoretical Extension of the Leader Trait Paradigm," *Leadership Quarterly* (December 2009): 855–75.

Khurana, R., *Searching for a Corporate Savior: The Irrational Quest for Charismatic CEOs*. Princeton, NJ: Princeton University Press, 2002.

Raelin, J.A., "The Myth of Charismatic Leaders," *Training & Development* (March 2003): 47–54.

Truth 29

Emerson, R.E., "Power-Dependence Relations," *American Sociological Review* (1962): vol. 27, 31–41.

Mintzberg, H., *Power In and Around Organizations*. Upper Saddle River, NJ: Prentice Hall, 1983.

Truth 30

Bing, M.N., H.K. Davison, I. Minor, M.M. Novicevic, and D.D. Frink, "The Prediction of Task and Contextual Performance by Political Skill: A Meta-Analysis and Moderator Test," *Journal of Vocational Behavior* (October 2011): 563–77.

Blickle, G., J. John, G.R. Ferris, and T. Momm, "Fit of Political Skill to the Work Context: A Two-Study Investigation," *Applied Psychology* (April 2012): 295–322.

Chang, C-H, C.C. Rosen, and P.E. Levy, "The Relationship between Perceptions of Organizational Politics and Employee Attitudes, Strain, and Behavior: A Meta-Analytic Examination," *Academy of Management Journal* (August 2009): 779–801.

Farrell, D., and J.C. Petersen, "Patterns of Political Behavior in Organizations," *Academy of Management Review* (July 1982): 405.

Kapoutsis, I., A. Papalexandris, A. Nikolopoulos, W.A. Hochwarter, and G.R. Ferris, "Politics Perceptions as Moderator of the Political Skill-Job Performance Relationship: A Two-Study, Cross-National, Constructive Replication," *Journal of Vocational Behavior* (February 2011): 123–35.

Kilduff, M., D.S. Chiaburu, and J.I. Menges, "Strategic Use of Emotional Intelligence in Organizational Settings: Exploring the Dark Side," in A. Brief and B. Staw (eds.), *Research in Organizational Behavior* (2010): vol. 30, 129–52.

Pfeffer, J., "Don't Dismiss Office Politics—Teach It," *Wall Street Journal* (October 24, 2011): R6.

"Social Studies," *Bloomberg Businessweek* (June 14, 2010): 72–73.

Truth 31

Avey, J.B., T.S. Wernsing, and M.E. Palanski, "Exploring the Process of Ethical Leadership: The Mediating Role of Employee Voice and Psychological Ownership," *Journal of Business Ethics* (April 2012): 21–34.

Fulmer, R.M., "The Challenge of Ethical Leadership," *Organizational Dynamics* (August 2004): 307–17.

Isaacson, W., *Steve Jobs*. New York: Simon & Schuster, 2011.

Rost, J.C., "Leadership: A Discussion About Ethics," *Business Ethics Quarterly* (January 1995): 129–42.

Seidman, D., "The Case for Ethical Leadership," *Academy of Management Executive* (May 2004): 134–38.

van Knippenberg, D., D. De Cremer, and B. van Knippenberg, "Leadership and Fairness: The State of the Art," *European Journal of Work and Organizational Psychology* (2007): vol. 16, no. 2, 113–40.

Truth 32

Avolio, B.J., and S.S. Kahai, "Adding the 'E' to E-Leadership: How It May Impact Your Leadership," *Organizational Dynamics* (January 2003): 325–38.

Shriberg, A., "Effectively Leading and Managing a Virtual Team," *The Business Review* (Summer 2009): 1–2.

Zaccaro, S.J. and P. Bader, "E-Leadership and the Challenges of Leading E-Teams: Minimizing the Bad and Maximizing the Good," *Organizational Dynamics* (January 2003): 381–85.

Truth 33

House, R.J., M. Javidan, P. Hanges, and P. Dorfman, "Understanding Cultures and Implicit Leadership Theories Across the Globe: An Introduction to Project GLOBE," *Journal of World Business* (Spring 2002): 3–10.

"Military-Style Management in China," *Asia Inc.* (March 1995): 70.

Peterson, M.F., and J.G. Hunt, "International Perspectives on International Leadership," *Leadership Quarterly* (Fall 1997): 203–31.

Taras, V., P. Steel, and B.L. Kirkman, "Three Decades of Research on National Culture in the Workplace: Do the Differences Still Make a Difference?" *Organizational Dynamics* (July–September 2011): 189–98.

Truth 34

Kirschenbaum, H., and V.L. Henderson (eds.), *The Carl Rogers Reader*. New York: Houghton Mifflin, 1989.

Robbins, S.P., and P.L. Hunsaker, *Training in InterPersonal Skills: TIPS for Managing People at Work*, 6th ed. Upper Saddle River, NJ: Prentice Hall, 2012: 91–93.

Rogers, C.R., and R.E. Farson, *Active Listening*. Chicago, IL: Industrial Relations Center at the University of Chicago, 1976.

Truth 35

Grosser, T.J., V. Lopez-Kidwell, G. Labianca, and L. Ellwardt, "Hearing It Through the Grapevine: Positive and Negative Workplace Gossip," *Organizational Dynamics* (January–March 2012): 52–61.

Hirschhorn, L., "Managing Rumors," in L. Hirschhorn (ed.), *Cutting Back*. San Francisco: Jossey-Bass, 1983: 49–52.

Kurland, N.B., and L.H. Pelled, "Passing the Word: Toward a Model of Gossip and Power in the Workplace," *Academy of Management Review* (April 2000): 428–38.

McKay, B., "At Coke, Layoffs Inspire All Manner of Peculiar Rumors," *Wall Street Journal* (October 17, 2000): A1.

Michelson, G., A. van Iterson and K. Waddington, "Gossip in Organizations: Contexts, Consequences, and Controversies," *Group and Organization Management* (August 2010): 371–90.

Rosnow, R.L., and G.A. Fine, *Rumor and Gossip: The Social Psychology of Hearsay*. New York: Elsevier, 1976.

Truth 36

Tannen, D., *Talking from 9 to 5*. New York: William Morrow, 1995.

Tannen, D., "Talking Past One Another: 'But What Do You Mean?' Women and Men in Conversation," in J.M. Henslin (ed.), *Down to Earth Sociology: Introductory Readings,* 12th ed. New York: Free Press, 2003: 175–81.

Tannen, D., *You Just Don't Understand: Women and Men in Conversation*. New York: Ballentine Books, 1991.

Truth 37

Bandura, A., *Social Learning Theory*. Upper Saddle River, NJ: Prentice Hall, 1977.

Truth 38

Millken, F.J., E.W. Morrison, and P.F. Hewlin, "An Exploratory Study of Employee Silence: Issues That Employees Don't Communicate Upward and Why," *Journal of Management Studies* (September 2003): 1453–76.

Mornell, P., "The Sounds of Silence," *INC.* (February 2001): 117–18.

Pinder, C.C., and K.P. Harlos, "Employee Silence: Quiescence and Acquiescence as Responses to Perceived Injustice," in G.R. Ferris (ed.), *Research in Personnel and Human Resources Management,* vol. 21. Greenwich, CT: JAI Press, 2001: 331–69.

Pinder, C.C., and K.P. Harlos, "Silent Organizational Behavior," paper presented at the Western Academy of Management Conference. March 2000.

Truth 39

Coker, B.L.S., "Freedom to Surf: The Positive Effects of Workplace Internet Leisure Browsing," *New Technology, Work, and Employment* (November 2011): 238–47.

"Digital Interruptions Resulting in Loss of Productivity, According to Survey by Social E-Mail Software Firm," *Telecomworldwide (May 18, 2011)*, www.telecomworldwide.com.

"Distracted," *Canadian Business* (August 16–September 12, 2011): 28–30.

Field, A., "Turning Off Email, Turning Up Productivity," *Workforce* (February 29, 2012), www.workforce.com.

Jett, Q.R., and J.M. George, "Work Interrupted: A Closer Look at the Role of Interruptions in Organizational Life," *Academy of Management Review* (July 2003): 494–507.

"Productivity Costs: Collaboration, Social Tools Cost $10,375 Per Person Annually in Lost Productivity," *The Controller's Report* (August 2011), www.iofm.com.

Sussman, S., N. Lisha, and M. Griffiths, "Prevalence of the Addictions: A Problem of the Majority or the Minority?" *Evaluation & the Health Professions* (March 2011): 3–56.

Wajcman, J., and E. Rose, "Constant Connectivity: Rethinking Interruptions at Work," *Organization Studies* (July 2011): 941–61.

Truth 40

Campion, M.A., E.M. Papper, and G.J. Medsker, "Relations between Work Team Characteristics and Effectiveness: A Replication and Extension," *Personnel Psychology* (Summer 1996): 429–52.

Cohen, S.G. and D.E. Bailey, "What Makes Teams Work: Group Effectiveness Research from the Shop Floor to the Executive Suite," *Journal of Management* (June 1997): 239–90.

Hackman, J.R., *Leading Teams: Setting the Stage for Great Performance*. Boston: Harvard Business School Press, 2002.

Hinds, P.J., K.M. Carley, D. Krackhardt, and D. Wholey, "Choosing Work Group Members: Balancing Similarity, Competence, and Familiarity," *Organizational Behavior and Human Decision Processes* (March 2000): 226–51.

Hyatt, D.E., and T.M. Ruddy, "An Examination of the Relationship between Work Group Characteristics and Performance: Once More into the Breach," *Personnel Psychology* (Autumn 1997): 553–85.

Mesmer-Magnus, J.R., and L.A. DeChurch, "Information Sharing and Team Performance: A Meta-Analysis," *Journal of Applied Psychology* (March 2009): 535–46.

Neuman, G.A., and J. Wright, "Team Effectiveness: Beyond Skills and Cognitive Ability," *Journal of Applied Psychology* (June 1999): 376–89.

Peeters, M.A.G., H.F.J.M. Van Tuijl, C.G. Rutte, and I.M.M.J. Reymen, "Personality and Team Performance: A Meta-Analysis," *European Journal of Personality* (August 2006): 377–96.

Stewart, G.L., and M.R. Barrick, "Team Structure and Performance: Assessing the Mediating Role of Intrateam Process and the Moderating Role of Task Type," *Academy of Management Journal* (April 2000): 135–48.

Truth 41

Comer, D.R., "A Model of Social Loafing in Real Work Groups," *Human Relations* (June 1995): 647–67.

Karau, S.J. and K.D. Williams, "Social Loafing: A Meta-Analytic Review and Theoretical Integration," *Journal of Personality and Social Psychology* (October 1993): 681–706.

Latane, B., K. Williams, and S. Harkins, "Many Hands Make Light the Work: The Causes and Consequences of Social Loafing," in J.M. Levine and R.L. Moreland (eds.), *Small Groups*. New York: Psychology Press, 2006: 822–32.

Liden, R.C., S.J. Wayne, R.A. Jaworski, and N. Bennett, "Social Loafing: A Field Investigation," *Journal of Management* (April 2004): 285–304.

Murphy, S.M., S.J. Wayne, R.C. Liden, and B. Erdogan, "Understanding Social Loafing: The Role of Justice Perceptions and Exchange Relationships," *Human Relations* (January 2003): 61–84.

Truth 42

Guzzo, R.A. and G.P. Shea, "Group Performance and Intergroup Relations in Organizations," in M.D. Dunnette and I.M. Hough (eds.), *Handbook of Industrial & Organizational Psychology*, 2nd ed., vol. 3. Palo Alto, CA: Consulting Psychologists Press, 1992: 288–90.

Jackson, S.E., K.E. May, and K. Whitney, "Understanding the Dynamics of Diversity in Decision Making Teams," in R.A. Guzzo and E. Salas (eds.), *Team Effectiveness and Decision Making in Organizations*. San Francisco: Jossey-Bass, 1995: 204–61.

Joshi, A., and H. Roh, "The Role of Context in Work Team Diversity Research: A Meta-Analytic Review," *Academy of Management Journal* (June 2009): 599–627.

Watson, W.E., K. Kumar, and L.K. Michaelsen, "Cultural Diversity's Impact on Interaction Process and Performance: Comparing Homogeneous and Diverse Task Groups," *Academy of Management Journal* (June 1993): 590–602.

Truth 43

Greenberg, J., "Equity and Workplace Status: A Field Experiment," *Journal of Applied Psychology* (November 1988): 606–13.

Headlam, B., "How to E-Mail Like a C.E.O.," *New York Times Magazine* (April 8, 2001): 7–8.

Rubin, M., "Group Status Is Related to Group Prototypicality in the Absence of Social Identity Concerns," *The Journal of Social Psychology* (2012): vol. 152, no. 3, 386–89.

Truth 44

Diskell, J.E., G.F. Goodwin, E. Salas, and P.G. O'Shea, "What Makes a Good Team Player? Personality and Team Effectiveness," *Group Dynamics: Theory, Research, and Practice* (December 2006): 249–71.

Prieto, J., "The Team Perspective in Selection and Assessment," in H. Schuler, J.L. Farr, and M. Smith (eds.), *Personnel Selection and Assessment: Industrial and Organizational Perspectives*. Hillsdale, NJ: Erlbaum, 1994: 221–34.

Sinclair, A., "The Tyranny of a Team Ideology," *Organization Studies* (1992): vol. 13, no. 4, 611–26.

Truth 45

DeDreu, C.K.W. and L.R. Weingart, "Task Versus Relationship Conflict, Team Performance, and Team Member Satisfaction: A Meta-Analysis," *Journal of Applied Psychology* (August 2003): 741–49.

Jehn, K.A., "A Qualitative Analysis of Conflict Types and Dimensions in Organizational Groups," *Administrative Science Quarterly* (September 1997): 530–57.

Jehn, K.A. and E.A. Mannix, "The Dynamic Nature of Conflict: A Longitudinal Study of Intragroup Conflict and Group Performance," *Academy of Management Journal* (April 2001): 238–51.

Nemeth, C.J., J.B. Connell, J.D. Rogers, and K.S. Brown, "Improving Decision Making by Means of Dissent," *Journal of Applied Social Psychology* (January 2001): 48–58.

Robbins, S.P., *Managing Organizational Conflict: A Nontraditional Approach*. Upper Saddle River, NJ: Prentice Hall, 1974.

Shaw, J.D., J. Zhu, M.K. Duffy, and K.L. Scott, "A Contingency Model of Conflict and Team Effectiveness," *Journal of Applied Psychology* (March 2011): 391–400.

Truth 46

Janis, I.L., *Groupthink: Psychological Studies of Policy Decisions and Fiascoes*, 2nd ed. Boston: Houghton Mifflin, 1982.

Moorhead, G., R. Ference, and C.P. Neck, "Group Decision Fiascos Continue: Space Shuttle Challenger and a Revised Groupthink Framework," *Human Relations* (May 1991): 539–50.

Park, W., "A Review of Research on Groupthink," *Journal of Behavioral Decision Making* (July 1990): 229–45.

Park, W.W., "A Comprehensive Empirical Investigation of the Relationships among Variables of the Groupthink Model," *Journal of Organizational Behavior* (December 2000): 873–87.

"United States Senate Select Committee on Intelligence: Report on Pre-Iraq War Intelligence," CBC News Online, July 9, 2004, www.cbc.ca/news.

Truth 47

"100 Best Companies to Work For," *Fortune* (January 22, 2007): 80–88.

Barnett, R.C., and D.T. Hall, "How to Use Reduced Hours to Win the War for Talent," *Organizational Dynamics* (2001): vol. 29, no. 3, 192–210.

Cappelli, P., J. Constantine, and C. Chadwick, "It Pays to Value Family: Work and Family Tradeoffs Reconsidered," *Industrial Relations* (April 2000): 175–98.

Darcy, C., A. McCarthy, J. Hill, and G. Grady, "Work-Life Balance: One Size Fits All? An Exploratory Analysis of the Differential Effects of Career Stage," *European Management Journal* (April 2012): 111–20.

Ford, M.T., B.A. Heinen, and K.L. Langkamer, "Work and Family Satisfaction and Conflict: A Meta-Analysis of Cross-Domain Relations," *Journal of Applied Psychology* (January 2007): 57–80.

Oglesby, C., "More Options for Moms Seeking Work-Family Balance," cnn.com, May 10, 2001, www.cnn.com.

Truth 48

Fisher, R. and W. Ury, *Getting to Yes: Negotiating Agreement Without Giving In.* New York: Penguin Books, 1986.

Thompson, L., *The Truth About Negotiations.* Upper Saddle River, NJ: Prentice Hall PTR, 2008.

Truth 49

Behson, S.J., E.R. Eddy, and S.J. Lorenzet, "The Importance of the Critical Psychological States in the Job Characteristics Model: A Meta-Analytic and Structural Equations Modeling Examination," *Current Research in Social Psychology* (May 2000): 170–89.

Sims, H.P., and A.D. Szilagyi, "Job Characteristic Relationships: Individual and Structural Moderators," *Organizational Behavior and Human Performance* (June 1976): 211–30.

Sutherland, J., "Job Attribute Preferences: Who Prefers What?" *Employee Relations* (2011). vol. 33, no. 3, 193–221.

Wanous, J.P., "Individual Differences and Reactions to Job Characteristics," *Journal of Applied Psychology* (October 1974): 616–22.

Truth 50

Hackman, J.R., "Work Design," in J.R. Hackman and J.L. Suttle (eds.), *Improving Life at Work.* Santa Monica, CA: Goodyear, 1977: 132–33.

Truth 51

Burke, R.J., "Why Performance Appraisal Systems Fail," *Personnel Administration* (June 1972): 32–40.

Hite, B., "Employers Rethink How They Give Feedback," *Wall Street Journal* (October 13, 2008): B5.

Meyer, H.H., "A Solution to the Performance Appraisal Feedback Enigma," *Academy of Management Executive* (February 1991): 68–76.

Truth 52

Kelley, H.H., "Attribution in Social Interaction," in E. Jones et al (eds.), *Attribution: Perceiving the Causes of Behavior.* Morristown, NJ: General Learning Press, 1972: 1–26.

Truth 53

Plous, S., *The Psychology of Judgment and Decision Making.* New York: McGraw Hill, 1993.

Robbins, S.P., *Decide & Conquer: Making Winning Decisions and Taking Control of Your Life.* Upper Saddle River, NJ: Financial Times/ Prentice Hall, 2004.

Tversky, A. and D. Kahneman, "Judgment Under Uncertainty: Heuristics and Biases," *Science* (September 1974): 1124–31.

Truth 54

Brett, J.F., and L.E. Atwater, "360-Degree Feedback: Accuracy, Reactions, and Perceptions of Usefulness," *Journal of Applied Psychology* (October 2001): 930–42.

"Feedback, Feedback Everywhere…But How Effective Is the 360-Degree Approach?" *Training Strategies for Tomorrow* (November/ December 2002): 19–23.

Lepsinger, R. and A.D. Lucia, *The Art and Science of 360 Degree Feedback,* 2nd ed. San Francisco: Pfeiffer, 2009.

Maylett, T., "360-Degree Feedback Revisited: The Transition from Development to Appraisal," *Compensation and Benefits Review* (September/October 2009): 52–59.

Peiperl, M.A., "Getting 360 Feedback Right," *Harvard Business Review* (January 2001): 142–47.

Truth 55

Erwin, D.G., and A.N. Garman, "Resistance to Organizational Change: Linking Research and Practice," *Leadership & Organization Development Journal* (2010). vol. 31, no. 1, 39–56.

Nadler, D.A., "The Effective Management of Organizational Change," in J.W. Lorsch (ed.), *Handbook of Organizational Behavior.* Upper Saddle River, NJ: Prentice Hall, 1987: 358–69.

Oreg, S., and Y. Berson, "Leadership and Employees' Reactions to Change: The Role of Leaders' Personal Attributes and Transformational Leadership Style," *Personnel Psychology* (Autumn 2011): 627–59.

Stebel, P., "Why Do Employees Resist Change?" *Harvard Business Review* (May–June 1996): 86–92.

Truth 56

Cotton, J.L., *Employee Involvement.* Newbury Park, CA: Sage, 1993.

Erwin, D.G., and A.N. Garman, "Resistance to Organizational Change: Linking Research and Practice," *Leadership & Organization Development Journal* (2010). vol. 31, no. 1, 39–56.

Giangreco, A., and R. Peccei, "The Nature and Antecedent of Middle Manager Resistance to Change: Evidence from an Italian Context," *The International Journal of Human Resource Management* (October 2005): 1812–29.

Kotter, J.P. and L.A. Schlesinger, "Choosing Strategies for Change," *Harvard Business Review* (March–April 1979): 106–14.

Lines, R., "Influence of Participation in Strategic Change: Resistance, Organizational Commitment and Change Goal Achievement," *Journal of Change Management* (September 2004): 193–215.

Truth 57

Abelson, M., and B. Baysinger, "Optimal and Dysfunctional Turnover: Towards an Organizational Level Model," *Academy of Management Review* (April 1984): 331–41.

"Accounting for Good People," *Economist* (July 21, 2007): 73–75.

Dalton, D.R., W.D. Todor, and D.M. Krackhardt, "Turnover Overstated: The Functional Taxonomy," *Academy of Management Review* (January 1982): 117–23.

Glebeek, A.C., and E.H. Bax, "Is High Employee Turnover Really Harmful? An Empirical Test Using Company Records," *Academy of Management Journal* (April 2004): 277–86.

Hollenbeck, J.R., and C.R. Williams, "Turnover Functionality versus Turnover Frequency: A Note on Work Attitudes and Organizational Effectiveness," *Journal of Applied Psychology* (November 1986): 606–11.

Jones, D., "More Firms Cut Workers Ranked at Bottom to Make Way for Talent," *USA Today* (May 30, 2001): 1B.

Truth 58

Datta, D.K., J.P. Guthrie, D. Basuil, and A. Pandev, "Causes and Effects of Employee Downsizing: A Review and Synthesis," *Journal of Management* (January 2010): 281–348.

"Layoff 'Survivor' Stress: How to Manage the Guilt and the Workload," *HR Focus* (August 2009): 4–6.

Noer, D.M., *Healing the Wounds*. San Francisco, CA: Jossey-Bass, 1993.

Robbins, S.P., "Layoff-Survivor Sickness: A Missing Topic in Organizational Behavior," *Journal of Management Education* (February 1999): 31–43.

Truth 59

Gibson, J.W., and D.V. Tesone, "Management Fads: Emergence, Evolution, and Implications for Managers," *Academy of Management Executive* (November 2001): 122–33.

Jackson, B., *Management Gurus and Management Fashions: A Dramatistic Inquiry*. London: Routledge, 2001.

McGill, M.E., *American Business and Quick Fix*. New York: Henry Holt, 1988.

Rousseau, D.M., and S. McCarthy, "Educating Managers from an Evidence-Based Perspective," *Academy of Management Learning & Education* (March 2007): 84–101.

Staw, B.M., and L.D. Epstein, "What Bandwagons Bring: Effects of Popular Management Techniques on Corporate Performance, Reputation, and CEO Pay," *Administrative Science Quarterly* (September 2000): 523–56.